I SEE A NEW
AMERICA

RICK JOYNER

I See a New America
by Rick Joyner
Copyright © 2011
Trade Edition

International Standard Book Number— 978-1-60708-403-7; 1-60708-403-1

Published by Quest Ventures
375 Star Light Drive, Fort Mill, SC 29715

Distributed by Morningstar Publications, Inc.
375 Star Light Drive, Fort Mill, SC 29715
www.morningstarministries.org
1-800-542-0278

Distributed by The Oak Initiative
375 Star Light Drive, Fort Mill, SC 29715
1-803-547-8217
www.theoakinitiative.org

Cover Design: Kevin Lepp
Book Layout: Dana Zondory

Unless otherwise indicated, all Scripture quotations are taken from the New American Standard Bible, copyright © 1960, 1962, 1963, 1968, 1971, 1973, 1974, 1977 by The Lockman Foundation. Italics in Scripture are for emphasis only.

CONTENTS

CHAPTER ONE

AMERICA IN TEN YEARS

What will America be like in ten years? Predictions vary, but presently virtually everyone seems to think that America is in decline. This thought is not new. Detractors have been saying this since America ascended in prominence and power, especially when we entered an economic slump. So far we have always rebounded stronger than ever. Will we do it again?

Choose Your Destiny

No doubt the slump we are presently in seems different. We have been told for some time that we are climbing out of it, and the stock market seemed to be reflecting this, but almost all of the economic indicators say some things are still very wrong, which we will address. We cannot win the great challenges of our times if we do not understand them. Even so, America's best times can be in our future. What is threatening to be our doom can be overcome, and if we learn the lessons that got us into this mess, it can be a springboard for a new beginning.

The present crises we're facing as a nation are in some ways more dangerous than any we've faced before because they have been caused by our own foolishness. They remain dangerous because so few understand them. An enemy in your face can be much easier to deal with than one you cannot see. The roots of our biggest problems have yet to be given even a brief mention by our leaders, so ignorance is still our biggest enemy.

The thesis of this book is that not only can we rebound from the present decline; we can come out of it greater and stronger than ever. The key word is that we "can." Whether we do or not depends on us. If we can peer through the fog of the present problems, we are standing at the greatest potential for advancement we've ever had. No other nation on earth has the foundation or the potential that America has right now.

We are in a crisis, and we need some radical surgery, but when we get past it, we can go much higher and much further. If we continue to decline, it is because we gave up, not because it was inevitable. We can choose our destiny. There are encouraging signs that Americans are starting to wake up, which is the most important barometer we should watch.

My hope has a strong foundation, but part of this is my belief in America's willingness to face and overcome some ultimate issues. We cannot downplay the seriousness of these times. This book was written for those who have the courage and maturity to want to see our situation, as difficult as it is, with faith and resolve, not just looking at problems as obstacles but as opportunities. We have a choice, and we have an opportunity, but we must get engaged. It is the time for action.

One of the definitions for crisis is "the point in a disease when it is determined if a patient will live or die." At this writing, the stock market is up and corporate profits are up. Even so, America is still in a crisis, and will be until some fundamental issues threatening us have been identified and corrected. We have had a series of national heart attacks. This can be the beginning of the end, or it can wake us up to some changes we need to make that will leave us healthier than ever, with a much longer life ahead of us. All that has happened in the last few years can work out for our good if we correct what caused the economic heart attacks.

Many more Americans are grasping the crisis and are standing up with resolve to make the needed changes. Neither are they being deceived by temporary reprieves or doctored data. This is a most encouraging sign. We must have faith, but we must have real faith based on truth and reality. Americans are getting more educated and discerning on the current issues than possibly any time in our history as well. This has caused many to become disillusioned with our government, which means to lose our illusions, and this is a good thing. We can again have a government that is of the people, by the people, and for the people, even though in recent times we have drifted from this.

Studies on the tipping points, which brought radical changes to civilization, have determined that the number of people required for this is as few as the square root of 1% of the population. This means that as few as one hundred people can bring profound transformation to a population of a million. Carry it out and this means that as few as thirty thousand devoted people can radically transform America. Many times this number are now arising in America with resolve to see transformation. There is great hope for our future!

The Devil's Prophecies

Of course, the tipping-point principle can be used for evil as well as good. This is why groups that represent a small percentage of the population have been able to radically impact our culture. Many, even some of our own citizens, would be happy to see America collapse. We are in a great struggle, and it is not possible to win such a struggle without understanding who and what we are struggling against. To begin to understand our challenge, let's look at what the prophets of doom are saying about America's future.

#1 Our days as a superpower are at an end. Many countries are betting that America is too exhausted from continuous wars to carry the weight of being a superpower much longer, and many Americans do not want to carry this burden any longer. There are, no doubt, signs of national exhaustion.

There are also signs of American revival and rejuvenation. We are still in a position to remain the dominant power on earth for many years to come if we so choose. This is still in our power to choose, but we must have the national will to want it. If you do not think this is important, just take a few minutes to consider what the world would be like today if there had not been an America.

#2 America will break up like the former Soviet Union did into four or more smaller nations. This is a favorite of Russian pundits as we might expect, but there is also some basis for this potential. The disregard for the Constitution has caused many states to consider, or to have actually passed, legislation that could lead toward this.

Another path could also lead us to an even stronger union. We are at a crossroads, and I will have more to say about this later.

#3 America will meld into a semi-socialist state like the European model. Many see this as preferable, but America does not do "middle of the road" well, and so this would likely result in the breakup of the union. The tension between those who want to take America down this road and those who would refuse to go that way is growing. This is one reason for the increasing strain between the left and right in Washington. We are at a crossroads, and a clear direction will soon have to be chosen.

#4 A meltdown of our economy will be followed by anarchy for a period. Then a totalitarian dictatorship will fill the vacuum. This is more likely than the slide into a European-type semi-socialist state. The crash of the dollar could throw America into unprecedented economic chaos, and recent decisions by our government will keep us hanging over this cliff if there is not a clear turning away from deficit spending.

Americans are getting this. Increasing numbers seem resolved to hold the government accountable, and the 2010 elections were a great sign they will not back down. The future of the

Republican Party may rest on it waking up and doing what it has claimed to be for—smaller government, a balanced budget, and responsible spending by government. Such a turn could lead us back toward safety and stability. Remove erratic government policy and leadership, and the American economy is still the strongest in the world by a great margin.

#5 Islamic jihadists believe America will be destroyed. These are obviously seeking to make their prophecy come true. The openly publicized strategy of jihadists in America to use political correctness and our own Constitution against us has been so successful they are now considering America as possibly the easiest prey ever. Most Americans still consider this preposterous, especially since Muslims only make up a small percentage of the population. That is what the Czarists in Russia thought about the Bolsheviks too, since just 20,000 Bolsheviks were able to seize power over a nation of millions. It is a basic military principle that you must see the enemy in order to defeat them, and America has been blind to this very real threat.

Even so, there are signs of Americans awakening to this now. Books on Islam and the strategy of the Muslim Brotherhood are starting to rise on the bestseller lists, indicating Americans are now resolved to throw off the deception and fight this sworn enemy of America and Western civilization. Exposure to the light is the main thing that breaks the power of darkness, and as the light continues to shine on this threat, it can be greatly reduced.

Above are the five most popular predictions about the future of America. They are sobering, but we need to be sobered by the times we're in. It sometimes takes a slap in the face to wake up.

If we wake up, none of these will come to pass, but on the contrary, our best days will be in our future, not our past. America can be much stronger than ever in virtually every way. There are signs that we are starting to turn in the direction that will take us to a very bright future.

I see a new America, better than ever, still ascending and remaining the most powerful and prosperous nation on earth for long into the future. We can also use this power and prosperity to help elevate the rest of the world. America is not the New Jerusalem, and it is not the kingdom of God, but it has a part in helping to prepare the way for them.

To rise and not fall, we cannot deny our great and pressing problems. These are so serious that they threaten to destroy our entire political and economic system. Others are tearing away at the basic moral fabric of America. Even so, just as the Chinese word for crisis is the same word for opportunity, these crises/opportunities are now so large and threatening that they are forcing us to find answers to ultimate issues. It is in the answers that we will have the opportunity to build a future that is even brighter than our history.

Our Greatest Need

Embracing the great challenges now facing us will strengthen us. There is growing evidence that the American people are ready to take on these great challenges. Many Americans are tired, but many others are getting a second wind, and even the tired can be rejuvenated. *Our greatest need is for a new breed of leadership to refocus our energy and potential.*

To make it through the coming times, we will need a leadership with the vision, character, fortitude, and resolve of a George Washington or an Abraham Lincoln. Such leadership does not walk the earth often, and they may not seem apparent at this time. In Scripture, good leaders are a blessing from God. Poor, immature leadership is one of the worst curses that can come upon a nation. We need God's favor, but both Scripture and history reveal that He is always ready to extend it to a nation that will turn to Him.

We are at a watershed moment in history. Great change is coming, and great leadership is required. Such times present the greatest opportunity for either good or evil. We are precariously close to evil prevailing, but America has been in crises before, and great leaders arose to lead through them. Our most desperate need is for a different type of leadership than we have had for a very long time. We are commanded in the New Testament to pray for our leaders, and this should be a primary prayer at this time. Don't just lament the bad, but start praying for and expecting better.

The following vision of where we can go as a nation is very real and very doable. In just ten years, America could have:

- The strongest and most secure economy in the world
- Virtually full employment
- The most productive and efficient manufacturing in the world
- A balanced Federal budget
- No national debt
- Independence from foreign energy
- Virtually no pollution
- The best, most affordable, and available healthcare system in the world
- The best and most affordable education system in the world
- The most powerful, effective defense that provides security for our country and stability for the world
- A welfare system that takes care of the truly needy with dignity
- A Social Security system that honors seniors, allowing them all to live in the dignity, respect, and security they deserve
- More freedom
- Negligible crime
- A foreign policy that elevates the rest of the world, while discouraging and inhibiting the dangerous ambitions of rogue states and terrorists.

Sound impossible? Sound like some utopian dream? All of this is not only possible but within our reach. We should not settle for less.

We can do this, but to save our nation and lay the foundation for the future that we are capable of is going to require the same kind of courage, boldness, and willingness to sacrifice that led to our founding as a nation. It's now our turn. Will we rise to the occasion?

This does not have to be the beginning of our decline, but the beginning of a new and brighter future. We need the vision to see this and then the resolve to see it come true. For more than two hundred years, America has been the most interesting and dynamic nation on earth. From the great innovations to world-impacting movements and cultural changes, one new idea after another has come from America. Most have been a benefit to the world. It is not time for this to end. It is time for a new beginning.

America has faced some of the world's biggest issues and challenges in the past and found solutions to them. The solutions were not always perfect, and many can still use improvement, but no nation has accomplished as much in as many fields as America has over the last two hundred years. "The American experiment" has worked. It's not time to end it; rather it is time to benefit from all that we've learned.

We are a nation of kinetic energy, and it is our nature to be in motion. There are obviously things we can do better, and so continual improvement is necessary; however, some things should not be changed. The love of adventure, or pressing the outer limits, is one of them. There is much more adventure left in America and for America.

The remainder of this book defines and explores many of the great challenges America is now facing. It takes some courage just to examine them, and even more to overcome them. Every time America has faced such seemingly overwhelming challenges, she has proven well able to overcome them because courage and resolve are two of our greatest resources. We can do this.

CHAPTER TWO
YOU ARE HERE

If you have ever gone to a large shopping mall looking for a certain store, you probably went to the map that gives the layout of the stores. That map would not do any good without the big star that says "You are HERE." This is our first goal, to establish where we are so that we can see the best path to where we want to go.

The most basic structure of a nation or culture is not its government but its economy. You can have no government and still have an economy, but you cannot have a government without an economy. Government makes and enforces the rules of the economy, but the economy is the game. The economy is not the only thing, but it is the main glue for all of the other social factors.

The economy is where the most basic human transactions take place, so it can reveal more about the characteristics and the character of a nation or culture than possibly anything else. The fact that the American economy has been the most vibrant and exciting in the world for a long time reflects the energy, excitement, and adventure that is the American culture. We have hit some bumps in the road, and even turned up some box canyons and had to retrace our steps a few times, but the progress made has been unparalleled in history. The pioneering spirit is still very much basic to our nature and a key to our progress.

Economies reveal much about a nation or people and are easy to understand if we know just a few of the basic principles. Once we start to grasp these, the message can be most interesting. We will take a look at what our economy tells us about ourselves, but first let's take a general overview of history. Seeing how the world got to where we are is crucial to really understanding our present circumstances and the most powerful forces now influencing and, to some degree, controlling the world.

The Four Powers of the Earth

Four powers influence or control the world. These are 1) Military, 2) Religious, 3) Political, and 4) Economic. Just a basic understanding of these and their interrelationships can give us a good understanding of our history, the present world, and where present trends are leading us. We will examine each of them briefly in the sequence in which they gained ascendancy in civilization.

The First Great Power—Military

There have been four major epochs in human history. The first was the Military epoch. In this age, the most powerful leaders in the world were Military leaders, the conquerors such as Pharaoh, Nebuchadnezzar, Alexander the Great, and the Caesars. This period lasted from the beginning of recorded history until about 300 A.D. During this period, almost all wars and conflicts were about conquest.

The Second Great Power—Religion

The next great civilization-wide epoch was dominated by Religion. During this period, the Military powers became subservient to the emerging Religious powers such as Islam in the Middle East, Hinduism and Buddhism in the Far East, and Catholicism and Protestantism in the West. This is not so much about personal faith as it is about institutional Religion that became a dominant influence over civilization at the time. This period began to emerge about 300 A.D. and reached its peak during the Crusades and the apex of the

Ottoman Empire. Virtually all of the great wars and conflicts during this period were Religious wars, and the most powerful men in the world were Religious leaders.

The Third Great Power—Politics

The next great epoch of civilization was dominated by Politics. This period began about the time of the signing of the Magna Carta and continued through the mid-twentieth century. This was the time of great political changes, when new forms of government were born. There were great social upheavals such as the French, American, and Bolshevik revolutions, which were mostly about Political power and creating new forms of government. During this time, the most powerful men on earth were Political leaders, and both the Religious and Military powers became subservient to Political powers. Some were both Political and Military leaders such as Napoleon, or Political and Religious leaders like Wilberforce, but Politics was the preeminent power of this time.

Some Religious wars and wars of conquest occurred during this period, but most of the wars during this age were Political conflicts. Clausewitz wrote in his classic book, *On War,* that war is the attempt by one nation to impose its Political will on another nation. This was true during his period, but in the previous epoch most wars were an attempt of one Religion to impose its Religion on others. Previous wars of that age were simply about conquest and imposing one's culture on others.

The Fourth Great Power—Economics

The transitional times between these epochs were general and would sometimes take hundreds of years to make the transition; however, near the beginning of the 20th century we began to shift into a whole new era in which the most powerful force in the world was Economic power. The Bolshevik Revolution was both a Political and Economic revolution, marking the beginning of this great shift of powers. World War II was a Military, Political, and Economic war.

Japan attacked the U.S. because of our Economic boycott. Since then most wars and conflicts have been economically-motivated. The most powerful leaders in the world are now Economic leaders with the Military, Religious, and Political leaders becoming subservient to them. This is not to imply that it is the way it should be, but that this is in fact the way it is.

The Cold War was a very real war, but it was an Economic war. The great battles of the Cold War were not fought by generals as much as by bankers and corporate leaders in the West and leaders of industries in the East—the Economic leaders of the time. The Cold War was not won by our Military, or even our Political leadership, as much as it was by Wall Street. Most of the attention was on the Political and Military leaders during this contest, and even they seemed to only superficially understand that they were just a sideshow to the real conflict. Trying to keep up with the powerful economic engine of Western capitalism and free enterprise is what defeated communism.

If Clausewitz were writing today, he would say that war is the attempt of a nation to impose its Economic will on others. Military wars were ultimately the failure of the dominant powers of the times. Religious wars were ultimately the failure of the Religious leadership of their time. Political wars were ultimately the failure of Political leadership of that time. Likewise, most wars in this time, whether Military or Economic, were the failure of our Economic leadership.

This is not a theological study, but it is noteworthy that in the biblical prophecies about the end of this age one of the great tests is "the mark of the beast." This mark is an economic mark that determines who can buy, sell, and trade in the system of the times. Those who follow evil in this time are those who take the mark of the beast. However, the mark is not the evil; it is just evidence that those who have it worship the beast and not the Lord. As we understand the unfolding of history in the light of the four great powers of the earth, this mark starts to make more sense. In each of these ages, there was a great struggle to determine whether good or evil would dominate. In some places evil would prevail, and in some, good. The great struggle of these times is between good and evil Economic powers.

There are still Military, Religious, and Political wars and conflicts happening, but the motives for these are often masking Economic motives. Too often we have witnessed nations with tenuous leadership because economic problems try to shore up their position with an external conflict. We may also think of Islamic jihadists as Religious warriors, but jihad is about much more than a religion—it is about imposing Sharia Law on the nations, which is a totalitarian form of government and economy. We cannot fully understand the present world without understanding Islam, and especially Sharia Law, but since many outstanding books now address this important subject, we will not go any deeper with it here.

The most desirable condition is always peace. Economic wars may not seem as physically devastating as Religious wars, or as physically deadly, but they can be. Stalin's Economic war on the Ukraine is estimated to have killed twenty million people. Even so, if war becomes inevitable, you are at a great disadvantage if you do not go into it with a resolve to win. Just as with our Military defense, we should always seek peace, but be prepared for Economic war, and be both willing and able to execute it successfully if it comes to this.

Presently, America is still the greatest Economic power in the world and has the most powerful Military to defend it. We also have the most Political clarity and the strongest Religious foundation to support these. However, we have become increasingly vulnerable in these times because our Political leaders have had so little understanding of Economics—the dominant power of the age, which is where some of the most consequential battles are now being fought.

I've spent more than forty years studying history and economics, and it is my opinion that we have not had a President with a sufficient understanding of the economy in more than a century. Very few, if any, of our elected officials today understand the dominant power of the times we're in. The ones who understand the economy are too busy using that knowledge to want to be in government. This must change. The kind of leadership that has evolved in our government is so foreign to the real leaders of the times they do not want to have anything to do with it. We need government leaders who understand the times we live in and can move decisively in the real power centers of the world. If we do not understand these powers and control them, they will control us.

The Light Is Breaking Through

The good news is that many of the most brilliant Economic leaders of the times are American. Our challenge is to get them more engaged in the Political leadership of the nation, while maintaining a healthy respect for the other interests. We are not just an economy, but we are also engaged in some of the most important and compelling moral, social, religious, and political questions of the times as well. Even so, the Economic strength of America helps to give all of these a standing in the world they may not otherwise have.

Presently, America is where the most powerful Military, Religious, Political, and Economic powers are found. At this time, no other country on earth has the potential to impact the future like America has. If we do not use these powers, we will be used by them. We need strong, wise leadership that has an understanding of what has made America great and that can lead us. Then our extraordinary potential at this time can be fully utilized but with a strong moral compass.

CHAPTER THREE
THE BATTLE DEFINED

The premise of understanding the Economic age we are in is not to imply that Economics is more important than Religious, Political, or even Military issues. This is simply about impact—the ability to bring change on a national or international level. This is not a discussion of merit as much as power, and especially the power to impose change on others.

Even though we are in a new Economic age that we must understand and proactively engage, we can't neglect Military issues. Military conflict is life and death and will always require the greatest courage, and in many ways, the most challenging of all leadership. Therefore, we should always have the highest esteem for those who serve our nation in the military. Even so, we are in a war now, and defending our nation and our freedom can be in the hands of Economic leaders as much as our Military leaders.

Again, it is not possible to defeat an enemy you cannot see or understand. Seeing and understanding those who are working to defeat America economically is crucial if we are going to win the war we are now in. There was a reason why the worst attack on American soil in recent times was on the World Trade Center. That is what America is, the center of trade in the world. The defense of America now requires more than a Military defense—we also need a strong Economic defense. It's obvious that our present leaders' lack of understanding of the worldwide economic battle leaves us in the greatest jeopardy. Only if we understand what is happening can we take the necessary actions, and especially the preemptive action, which will save us from attacks and economic devastation.

Even though we started warning about the looming sub-prime crisis almost two years before it struck, the economic crisis that came upon us in 2008 was the result of an attack, not just the sub-prime foolishness. The crash of 2008 was not caused by market conditions, but as Representative Paul Kanjorski related on CSPAN after his briefing by The Federal Reserve, it was caused by someone pulling hundreds of billions out of the markets over the span of a couple of hours. The Fed reacted by pumping more than $100 billion into the market quickly, but it did not stop the slide, so they closed the trading window to prevent a complete crash of the markets. As Representative Kanjorski also related that day, "We came close to losing our entire economic and political systems."

We need to let that sink in. In one day, as most Americans went about their lives oblivious to anything significant even happening, we came close to losing our entire economy and political system—our democracy! This leads to some other important questions:

- How did we get into a situation where we could lose our entire economy and political system in a day?

- How do we get out of this situation?

- Who was it that pulled hundreds of billions out of our markets all at once, obviously intending to crash them?

- Why did they do this?

- What was the result of this obvious economic attack on our country?

That day we were hit by an economic nuclear bomb. Obviously, this was why President Bush was so visibly shaken and the reason he took the unprecedented step of calling for a suspension of the Presidential campaigns so McCain and Obama could come to Washington for a briefing on the crisis. Immediately, banks started shutting up like clams and have not fully opened again since. For those who understand the times, this attack was a more devastating attack than 9/11 and more like Pearl Harbor. We have not recovered from it yet. Why has this hardly been discussed publicly since?

Economic war may not do physical damage to us, at least not directly, but it can devastate a nation nearly as much as any military action could. Whoever attacked us in September 2008 did terrible damage to the country and continues to remain an enemy. We are obviously still blind to this enemy since not a single word has been said about who did this to us and why.

Once the enemy is identified and understood, the chances of defeating them are greatly increased. To just forget about this attack leaves us vulnerable to it happening again, and we are vulnerable.

Recognizing we are in an economic battle is a good start; understanding what to do about it is something completely different.

Back to the Future

Winston Churchill once said that our ability to see into the future was based on our knowledge of the past. This is true in virtually any field. We must have a solid foundational understanding of the past to understand the present. Then we can foresee and prepare for the future. This study is more about the present and future than the past, but to lay a solid foundation for these insights, we will occasionally look to history so we can grasp the basis of present trends.

One of the great encouragements that America is going to take the road to a bright future is the way that so many Americans are starting to pursue a better understanding of both history and the economy. Books on history, especially on the founding of our nation, have been rising on bestseller lists as well as books on the economy. You can now sit on a bus or in a diner and hear impressive conversations about the economy or the Constitution. Knowledge is illumination, or light, and the increase of knowledge is shining through a myriad of brilliant sources about the events and trends of our times.

Where Are We Going?

Understanding the economy is about more than just understanding markets. That's just one way we keep score, or see trends. The economy can tell us about what is really the heart and soul of a people. Almost every market indicator will tell us if people are optimistic because it will be reflected by the economy doing better. If a population starts having fears and doubts, the economy will begin to decline. This is not just faith in the economy, or the lack of it, but these are trends of basic optimism or doubt about life in general, as we will see.

The growing American interest in the economy is encouraging and can help us to build a stronger, more secure future. The next most important emerging factor is how the American people are learning to vet the information coming at them. In a time when reason has been muddled by relativism and political correctness, Americans are awakening to the fact that there is truth, and we can know it if we care enough to pursue it. Understanding the truth—the way things really are—will bring us clarity. We will then find the right road to a brighter future.

The Foundation

Foundations are important because the foundation holds up the entire building. The stronger a foundation is the more that can be built on it. America still has the strongest foundation in the world because of the strength of its four powers—Military, Religious, Political, and Economic. They are all under unrelenting attack at this time and have been damaged, but none is beyond repair and can be strong enough to continue building on far into the future.

An educated public was a major part of the strength of our foundations. America has also been a religious nation from the beginning, and to this day 90% of all Americans believe in God. About 85% of Americans consider themselves to be Christians, and an amazing 65% consider themselves to be "born again" Christians, or to have had a life-changing religious experience. Even so, from the beginning Americans have been very tolerant of other religions and the non-religious because of our core commitment to freedom. A major reason for this is because many of the first colonists were seeking religious freedom in order to escape from religious persecution.

Americans are religious, but they do not want to have religion imposed on them or to impose it on anyone else. True religion cannot be imposed. There can be no obedience if it is not possible to disobey. There can be no true worship unless there is the freedom not to worship. If God had just wanted everyone in line doing exactly what He wanted, He would have been much better off creating the computer than man and just programming the computers to do what He wanted. Like the God most Americans worship, Americans are devoted to freedom. This is a far stronger religious foundation than one that is imposed and that people are forced to embrace. Only volunteered religion will be from the heart. Anyone will try to break out of the jail of imposed religion and flee as fast as they can.

Not only did our forefathers want religious freedom badly enough to risk their lives to find it, they hated religious persecution enough to resolve to ensure the tolerant treatment of those who believed differently. So the freedom to have different religious convictions, or not have any, is a core American value. This is not to imply that there have not been times of religious persecution in America and that there is not even some happening now, but it is an aberration from what America was built on and is basically un-American.

Freedom of religion led to a devotion to all of our other basic freedoms. Freedom is the foundation of creativity and initiative—the most powerful of all economic engines as well as the foundation of American progress and prosperity. Work ethics also have been imparted by many of the religious movements in America that have salted the entire nation with a devotion to performance and accomplishment.

Regardless of how hard secularists have tried, they cannot possibly understand America without understanding religion in America. Most Europeans tend to have a basic misunderstanding of

America and Americans because even when they try to understand the religious foundations of America, they view it from their own religious experiences, which are very different from ours. I have been to Europe many times and have always read what they say about America and Americans while I am there. I have not yet read an article that I thought really understood either. The same is probably true of the way Americans view Europeans, or any other nation, but much of what is presumed about America is simply not accurate. We therefore cannot let them define us, but we do need to understand ourselves.

Modern democracy was born out of the Protestant Reformation in Switzerland, especially from the teachings of John Calvin. His teachings were intended for the church, to protect it from what he viewed as autocratic domination from Rome at the time. It is not likely even he could see all of the eventual consequences of his teachings, especially the revolutionary changes it wrought in civil government.

This is not a discussion on the theological merits of Calvin's teachings, but rather their impact, especially on America. The Pilgrims were Calvinists, as were the primary religious leaders of America through the Revolutionary period. Their impact is sown throughout our government and our economy. We cannot fully understand America, past or present, without understanding this influence.

Before the Protestant Reformation, the majority of Christians believed that salvation was institutional, or that your salvation was based on being a member of the institutional church. The main premise of the Protestant Reformation was that salvation was personal and that salvation was based on personal belief, not just membership in the institution of the church. This had a huge impact not only on religion but on all of life, creating a whole new and historically unprecedented value to the individual.

This also brought an unprecedented responsibility to the individual and led to the belief that government existed for the people, and not the other way around. That was the basic premise of the American Revolution. This influence continues to be the basis of our present devotion to individualism in America.

Certainly Religion and Politics are still great powers with great influence. Calvinism resulted in modern democracy. Democracy was seen as having the potential to bring peace between nations. In this they may have been onto something because to date no democracy has ever attacked another democracy militarily.

During our nation's early history, great waves of revival and awakening swept the colonies. They continued to move in waves upon the young nation at fortuitous times. Each one brought change, and we can trace the basic influence of much of what we are today to these changes that came with religious revivals and movements. The "revelation" that government existed for the people rather than the other way around came during the First Great Awakening. The roots of the abolitionist movements were the direct result of the Second Great Awakening led by men such as Charles Finney.

Without television, professional sports, or hardly any of the forms of entertainment that we have today, until recent times church services were one of the most interesting and anticipated times of the week. Religion's impact on life in America was profound, and its impact on the shaping of the nation was profound. It was said that in the1700s in America that attending virtually any church for six years was at least equal to a bachelor's degree. Sermons were rich, deep, and compelling, with oratory being highly esteemed.

Sermons also were the place where most citizens received their news and their understanding of the great issues of the times. The great speeches like Patrick Henry's "Give me liberty or give me death" were heard in churches. Often the great oratory in the legislatures and Congress were admittedly borrowed from sermons. There were newspapers, but the analysis of the news was almost exclusively in the churches and synagogues (mosques did not come until much later).

Following the trend of where people get their understanding of the times can be a revelation. A few decades ago, almost everyone received their news from a 30-minute summary once a day from one of the three major networks or from their local newspaper. Today the news sources are myriad, with the Internet and bloggers now surpassing the traditional news media as major sources for most Americans. We have an increasingly educated, engaged, and intelligent American public that is also becoming increasingly skilled at discerning the information they receive.

Economics may be the most dominant power of these times, but the battle for the future is being waged on many more fronts than this. What good is it to be wealthy if we are miserable and wretched? Moral relativism and political correctness has blurred the distinctions between good and evil for many, and the result has been a terrible depression. Those with moral and spiritual clarity are standing out more and more, and will continue to do so in the days to come, just as the Prophet Isaiah predicted:

Arise, shine; for your light has come, and the glory of the LORD has risen upon you.

For behold, darkness will cover the earth, and deep darkness the peoples; but the LORD will rise upon you, and His glory will appear upon you.

And nations will come to your light, and kings to the brightness of your rising (Isaiah 60:1-3).

Isaiah had an amazing amount to say about these times, but the recurring theme of his prophecy was that even though there will be times of great darkness, the light will win in the end. As we read above, ultimately the nations are going to turn to the light, not the darkness.

An active, engaged citizenry filled with moral and spiritual clarity can prevent economic collapse.

CHAPTER FOUR
NEW BREED THINKING

Change is inevitable. It is coming fast and getting faster. However, it does not have to be uncontrollable, unstable change. We can determine the course of our future, but if we do not take the initiative to control it, then it will control us.

Our government has been drifting left for a long time, but recently we were jerked hard to the left. Now there is rising pressure to turn back. Even so, the ship of state is very large, and any turn can have a huge impact on millions. We do not want someone at the helm who does not know how or where to steer it. We must determine where we want to go and ensure that this is where our leadership can and will take us.

Dangerous Change

An economic trend of boom and bust has existed for too long and is getting more extreme and more dangerous. This is not necessary. We can have continuous and stable change, as well as continuous and stable growth. The up-and-down, left-and-right trend can and must be stopped because it is becoming more dangerous with the fast moving times.

As a jet pilot, I learned that even if the engine instruments were staying within their parameters, if they began to oscillate, there was a serious problem. If not corrected, the engine may not just shut down, but it could explode. This has been happening in our economic engine, and the cause of the oscillations must be corrected. These oscillations simply are not necessary, and to a large degree, are the result of the lack of leadership or the wrong kind of leadership in the economy.

The boom trend went to an extreme in the 1920s, and was followed by an extreme bust. It was not until the mobilization of World War II began that our economy started getting traction again after that one. It did not have to take that long to get going, but government policies were working counter to a restart until then, just as ours have been since 2008. The present sluggishness that we're in is not necessary.

The encouragement we have this time is that in spite of so many counter-productive policies being imposed on the economy, it has been able to plod along and start to move again, at least to some degree. This is a reflection of just how strong and resilient our economy is. Reverse some of the policies and direction we've been going, and our economy will soar. If we learn the lessons well that the times are giving us, we can go higher than ever, and safely.

New Breed Education

As stated, we are in need of a new breed of leadership in government that understands America, understands the times, and understands our economy and the world economy. This is more than having knowledge. We can have a lot of knowledge and information but not have understanding. To be effective, we must take the information and interpret it accurately and then apply it correctly. Just as an engine instrument is only going to be as reliable as its source of information, or its calibration, if our knowledge is vast, but does not come from the right place, it may be misleading us about the real conditions.

We also need a new breed of teacher in our schools. Many of the principles taught in our business schools are running far behind the times. Some of the principles of economics still taught as fact have long ago been refuted and disproved. For this reason, some of the most educated people in economics are the most out of touch with the real world.

Regretfully, a formal education does not always lead to the truth or wisdom. One example of this is President Lula of Brazil. He has brought about one of the most extraordinary economic transformations of a major nation in history and only has a fourth grade education! How could this be? Actually, by not having the blinders often imposed by the present method of public education, he was able to view things from outside of traditional "schools of thought," and by this, see them more accurately. Thus, he was able to propose and implement solutions that no one else had seen or done before, and they worked brilliantly.

President Lula had education, but he was self-educated, getting his knowledge from experience in the real world. Because he got his education from the real world, he has had a remarkable impact on the real world. This may explain why so many of the great innovators and inventors of our times do not have much formal education.

This is not intended to belittle the value of education. Education is illumination, or light, and we need to have it to see through the darkness of confusion and chaos of the times. Education is the cornerstone of progress and prosperity, as well as our peace and security. Even so, a basic transformation of education is needed to make it relevant to the times and prepare students for the world they will live in.

Because education is one of my deepest passions personally, I have started schools, and with them sought to address some of the basic issues to help prepare students better for life, not just grades. One of my greatest concerns was how it seemed that our education system was producing graduates who have a hard time "thinking outside of the box." Thinking creatively is required to be successful in this fast-changing world. This was being hindered in many students because the education system that has evolved penalizes innovation and creativity while rewarding mediocrity.

Many educators realize change is needed, and calls for it are increasing. This is another encouragement that America is becoming engaged in what will enable us to continue in leadership in the times. We judge a tree by its fruit, and the fruit being produced by much of the American education system needs to be examined. We need to challenge the pressure to conform, and especially the pressure to conform to mediocrity rather than greatness. Mediocrity is contrary to the basic DNA of America.

Jon Amos Comenius is called "the father of modern education" and may still be the only true genius in that field. His innovations are numerous. He was the first one to use illustrations in books and coined the saying that "a picture is worth a thousand words." He made learning glorious and wonderful. He also warned vehemently about schools that could become "slaughterhouses of the mind" if they went a certain direction, the very direction many of ours have gone. Have you wondered why so many schools are now being designed and built to look like prisons? This is not just for security and keeping the wrong people out, but keeping the minds of our children locked down.

Without question, too much of our present education produces students who have a hard time thinking creatively, but there are exceptions. Many have run the gauntlet of our present schools and prevailed to be creative thinkers anyway. However, far too many are being crushed into molds so that they will just be good worker bees the rest of their lives.

Not that there is anything wrong with being a worker bee if the rest of the time you have a life, but too many have their life vision so sapped that they can do little more than sit as automatons in front of the television when they are not at their boring jobs. I do not want to lay all of the blame for couch potatoes and low impact people on the education system, but if learning was made as glorious and exciting as it really is, fewer people would no doubt be so addicted to that which is in fact sapping their lives.

The American DNA is to be pioneers and explorers, always pushing the envelope. True education will lead to a life of learning, pursuit, and accomplishment. If learning were made as exciting as it should be, then our education would be laying the foundation for a life in pursuit of knowledge and understanding, as well as experience. We should not stop learning until we stop breathing.

New Breed Economics

This subject requires far more attention than we can give it here, but it is a major factor in why America seems to be getting mired and sluggish, especially in relation to our national vision and purpose. In relation to the crises we're now facing, especially in the economy, it is not always the case but too often it is true that "those who can do, do, and those who can't do, teach." Those who have not had to do what they teach in the real world often impart a way of thinking that makes it hard to adjust to the fluid conditions of the real world. For this reason, our education system needs as much revamping as the government does, but we'll have to save that for another study.

Here we need to consider that the great economic minds of the times are not found in academia. Keynesian economics did work fairly well during the transitional period between the Political and Economic ages, and can still work well for a time with countries just emerging from communism or socialism. However, Keynesian economics becomes an anchor to a maturing economy, and there is a point where it will grind any economy to a halt. On the other hand, unrestrained supply-side economics can allow economies to roar ahead too fast, and without some control, can lead to dangerous crashes. There must be a proper balance of freedom and control for sustained, stable growth.

It is now estimated that the knowledge in scientific fields such as engineering is doubling every eighteen months. If it takes you four years to get a degree, and it is even taught by someone who is on the cutting edge of knowledge in their field when your course began, you will graduate far behind in current, cutting-edge knowledge. What you have learned can still be useful, giving you enough foundational understanding to be able to start grasping the higher knowledge. Even so, if the fields that our education are preparing us to work in are changing so fast, we need to consider how our education needs to be adapting to this.

A few years ago when I was speaking at the German university city of Tubingen, the driver assigned to me was a German prince and expert mathematician. I asked him about his specific mathematical focus, and he replied that it was in mathematical theory. When I asked him how the theories he was working on would be applied, he said he did not know, and in fact, they did not expect anyone to know how to apply them for about one hundred years! Some of the best German mathematical minds were that far ahead of practical application, but they kept going. Why? Many of the practical applications of such things as the Theory of Relativity are just now unfolding even though the theory itself is approaching a century in age. The Germans felt that they had to stay that far ahead to actually be practical.

The point is that knowledge is increasing so fast that we must start thinking of prophetic academics, prophetic economics, and government leadership that can see and proactively prepare for the future. Our present leaders are so overwhelmed by present conditions and crises that they have no time to look ahead. This has a lot to do with the system that has evolved in government, which is as stifling to creative and futuristic thinking as much of our educational system is. Such a lack of visionary leadership is now causing serious problems. As the speed of change continues to increase, this will be increasingly costly.

Even so, America may have the best foundation and culture for adapting to these fast-changing times and for developing a system of education and government that can thrive in them. Out of the present crisis there is still the potential for a new day to dawn. The American people are rising up with a determination to see change, the right kind of change. If we want good to prevail, we cannot wallow in remorse too long at the mistakes of the past. We must see the solutions that will get us through and resolve that we are going to leave our children a nation that is in even better shape than we received it.

CHAPTER FIVE
FREEING FREE ENTERPRISE

Economic prosperity is not just about making money—it's about making progress. True progress is making better things and making things better. Free enterprise and capitalism have worked because to be successful you have to make what people need or want, and it has to be a good value. We have the freedom to make it or not or to buy it or not. This is the simple genius of the free market economy, and it only works when the people are free to decide what they want or don't want.

The Future World Economy

The free market is dominating the world economy more than ever. With India and China now grasping and applying the basics of the free market, and Russia passing through some of its growing pains, the free market will without a doubt dominate the future. Socialistic economies that do not have an underpinning of natural resources such as energy sources will continue to fall behind, change, or disappear. As the Cold War proved, there is simply no way for socialism to compete with a free market economy.

The former communist countries are putting the pedal to the metal in developing free market economies while America has been trying to put the brakes on since the elections of 2008—and in some ways even trying to put the transmission in reverse. The rest of the world is looking at this in astonishment but are happy to pass us by.

The elections of 2010 gave a shot of adrenalin to our economy, but the extra weight that the American economy is now carrying is more than dangerous to our economic health—it is not sustainable.

It is understandable that after the world economic trauma of 2008, the whole world stepped back a bit to re-examine the road we're on. The mistakes that led to that trauma were hard to understand, but the countries that did make some adjustments got going again. One of these was China. Some huge problems with China's economy will start showing up soon if not corrected, but the Chinese have grasped some free market principles that America has been forgetting, to their benefit and to our pain.

After 2008, our government began to micromanage and steer the economy in a direction America will ultimately never go. Some countries might accept socialism without too much of a fight, but it is too foreign to America. Now the stress between the economy and the government has made it clear that much more transformation is needed in government than the economy, and new leadership, or renewed leadership, is inevitable.

More than anything we need leaders in government who understand America, the economy, and especially the American economy. The Internationalist's mentality is based on a way the world used to be, not the way that it is now. Internationalism is being left far behind by those who are on the cutting edge of the times. Nationalism actually works much better with the emerging modern world. Internationalism can only work by destroying the foundations on which America was built and where the emerging great and powerful countries of the world are now heading.

The present Economic age has brought about conditions where nations that are even in conflict probably will not want physical destruction of their enemy. In the Economic wars, one nation does want to beat the others and gain dominance over them, but they definitely do not want to destroy them because it destroys their future markets. The unfolding modern world conflict is about power and subjugation but not destruction. Jihad is the exception.

Professional politicians may be the one group that is the least likely to understand the emerging world, especially the Economic age. They are also the one group that is likely to think that they understand it much better than anyone else. Herein lies a great problem that must be resolved in America, and the Founding Fathers had the solution all along—our Republic cannot be composed of professional politicians but of community leaders who serve in government as a duty, not a profession.

Marxism is in basic conflict with the direction of the modern world, but we still have Marxists in our government. They may not even know they are Marxists because they may not know the source of the ideas. Most professional politicians have a shallow understanding of the economy and many other things they are seeking to impose their will on. This is true of those in both major parties in America.

My statement that we have many Marxists in our government is not intended to stir up the paranoia of the McCarthy era, a very dark time in our history we never want to repeat. Instead, it is an attempt to stir everyone to know the source of their beliefs and what has been revealed in history as the consequences of implementing them.

Freedom and Flowers

Marxism has proven repeatedly, and without an exception, to be the worst evil and bondage that can be imposed on any people. It has proven 100% of the time to only impoverish the people who embrace it. What it does to a nation is far worse than just economic strangulation—it basically destroys the human soul. Only the most blind, ignorant of history or evil-intentioned can continue to embrace it.

One train ride across Eastern Europe when it was under the yoke of communism was enough proof of this for anyone who could see. There was no color. Everything was drab gray, or brown, just like the people under its iron boot who became some of the saddest of all creatures. I never met a person living under communism who was not afraid to express himself or herself. Marxism cannot exist without totalitarian control, which has to use fear, intimidation, and secret police. It is the darkest form of oppression ever devised by men.

Just a couple of years after the Iron Curtain came down, the same Eastern Europe was possibly the most colorful place on earth. There seemed to be flower boxes in full bloom under every window. The houses and buildings were painted the most interesting and brilliant colors. The people actually wore colorful clothes again. After living under such oppression, the last thing they wanted to do was stand out, and when the souls were freed, it was wonderful to see them soar again. The people who had not even seemed alive before were suddenly interesting and full of laughter.

Those first days after the Iron Curtain came down were full of joy and wonder. It was just the beginning of a hard road to rebuild cultures and countries, but freedom is a beautiful thing. People who are free are inevitably interesting, compelling, and creative. Every nation, culture, and race is brilliant when it is free. We were created to be free, and every human being deserves freedom. Freedom does need a strong moral compass or it can open the door to corruption, but when the proper but limited restraints are in place, freedom cannot help but to promote interchange, commerce, and true prosperity—the elevating of people. The opposite of freedom is always tyranny.

Eastern Europe and Russia are still struggling to find their way now, but they are on the way to living in liberty. We must not forget the long and winding road America followed to find our way this far, and we are still facing major crises. They deserve time, and they deserve our help. We may at times need theirs too.

Some of the crises we're now facing are the result of unrestrained liberty that opened the door to greed and excess. Freedom is the most beautiful flower, but it is also delicate. Freedom requires responsibility, which means restraint and moderation. Let's learn our lessons, and let's give grace to others who are learning their lessons, but we must never lose our freedom.

For nearly a century now most of the high-impact people in the world were located in America. This was not because Americans are so much smarter or better, but because the freedom here allowed it. Presently, just a few people are pulling the strings on the world economy. Most are still Americans, but we are losing our place fast. We must become proactive in getting the right people in the right places while we still have the power to do this. This has to begin with people who understand freedom and are committed to it as a core value. They are also the only ones who can really understand the unfolding world economy—which is the free market.

The Federal Reserve

The Federal Reserve Bank is not just a major factor in the American economy, but in the world economy as well. How it works and where it gets its resources and power are still mysteries to most, even Congress. For this reason, Congressman Ron Paul has brought up many interesting questions and objections to the Federal Reserve. I do not necessarily agree with some of his assumptions about this, but I do think the questions have merit.

It is scary having so much economic power concentrated in this enigmatic and opaque organization that to date has resisted almost any government oversight. There is only one thing that is scarier than that—having Congress take over and try to do this job! This is not to say there may not be another alternative, but to date no one has come up with one that would not politicize the Federal Reserve's critical function in our economy, and it is no doubt a very critical function.

Some blame the Fed for our present economic problems, but in truth, the Fed has been very accurate about warning us of coming troubles and has at times been able to save us from our foolishness. The system may still need to be changed, but if so, it needs to be done carefully. Whether you like the Fed or not, it has saved us repeatedly from catastrophes created by foolish government leadership. Even so, for the Fed to have the power to save us the way that it has at times, it also has the power to cause major problems. This is a two-edged sword. It is worthy of deep discussion and research, but if we overreact, it could lead to much worse consequences.

In relation to the economy, we need leadership that has the wisdom to know when to move forward with focus, purpose, and momentum, and when to be deliberate and careful. Those in political or economic leadership can make brief and seemingly insignificant statements, causing a huge reaction in the markets and even affect world economic trends. Small actions can have huge consequences.

There are also times when the government must intervene aggressively in the markets, and timidity can be costly in those times. In a crisis, sometimes doing the wrong thing is still better than not doing anything because the most important thing of all is to show leadership. Even so, it is even better to have intervention that is right for the situation. This is why it is so crucial to now have government leadership that understands the economy and the markets, having the wisdom to know when, where, and how to take action that will affect it.

That our economy has done so well over the last few decades is a testament to the power of the free market, not to the brilliance of our government leadership. Our economy has become what it has to a large degree in spite of the government, not because of it. At times the government has helped, and at times it has hurt, but in balance, it has probably done more damage than good when it has intervened.

For this reason, it is easy to understand why President George W. Bush usually considered that no action was the best action, but this is not always the case as he found out the hard way at the end of his Presidency. Even so, the free market economy has not only survived; it remains powerful and poised to do even better.

Capitalism and Free Enterprise

Marxist strategy is to "never waste a crisis," and if you don't have one, create one. At least the first part of this philosophy has been borrowed by some of the world's most successful capitalists too. Because of their skill in this, they have also been accused of starting the crises, but such accusations come with almost any success in this world. Some of the greatest and most enduring fortunes were made during some of this nation's greatest crises.

Great business minds will see opportunity in just about any situation, and the greatest will see opportunity in even the worst of times. Some may be exploiting the situation or other people's misfortunes, but it does not mean they're trying to do that. They are just doing what they do—business. These are also the ones who tend to pull us out of the economic slowdowns and crises by their initiative and ingenuity. We can't discourage initiative.

Some believe that just as energy is never destroyed but only changes forms; likewise wealth is never destroyed but just changes hands. Higher physics acknowledges that this is not entirely true with energy, and it definitely is not true with wealth. Wealth can be destroyed, as Marxism has demonstrated in so many nations. Wealth can also be created, even when there may not be many natural resources, just by the power of ideas in the hands of those with the courage to act on them.

True wealth cannot be measured just in currency. As has been said, "Socialism distributes wealth, communism seizes wealth, but only capitalism creates wealth." This is also true if you substitute "capitalism" with "free enterprise." There is a difference between free enterprise and capitalism. With capitalism, you must have capital to have opportunity. With free enterprise, you only need initiative to have opportunity. It is free enterprise that creates wealth, which capitalism then manages—and grows it if it manages well.

You cannot have free enterprise without capitalism because if you win at the game of free enterprise, you must do something with your winnings, which is capital. The winners become capitalists to that degree. The more capitalists an economy has, the more people who have become winners. The healthiest economies will have an ever-increasing number of capitalists and yet learn how to keep the right balance between free enterprise and capitalism, always allowing for entry-level initiative.

Some are contending that capitalism is now dying, having run awry and led the world into its present dangerous and devastating problems. They have been saying this for well over a century, and with every crisis to date, capitalism has emerged stronger than ever. If the nations get control of the excesses and debt, which includes managing entitlements better, with Russia, China, and India entering the free markets, we are just entering what promises to be the golden age of capitalism.

Even though unrestrained capitalists are responsible for some of the great crises we are now facing, our greatest problems are not from capitalism. Unrestrained capitalism, or not properly regulated capitalism, can cause problems. However, capitalism will also be found at the root of the greatest economic and cultural advances of civilization. It needs guidance, but it also needs freedom. To find and keep the balance between these two is the solution to ultimate advancement, prosperity, and security. To keep capitalism renewing itself, it must have free enterprise. Presently, America has both, and with the best balance between them found in the world.

In history, we do not find a single example of a socialist nation having anything close to the kind of advancing and elevating of its people, or rising performance and productivity in its economy, as capitalism has produced wherever it is found. In every case, socialism has started a downward trend of performance and productivity, but capitalism an upward trend. There is a simple reason for this—capitalism promotes initiative and socialism inhibits it.

One of the great ironies of history is how former communist countries seem to understand this better than the West, which has enjoyed its benefits for so long. Because of this, former communist countries are starting to excel in capitalism to the point of challenging the West economically. Shockingly, the great nations of the West have been turning toward socialism! Those who endured the prison of communism and are just getting the hang of their new freedom stand in shock at what America is doing. However, there is now increasing evidence that Americans are waking up to the misdirection of recent times. The result is that a revival of the principles that made America so great for so long are being recovered.

The Birth of Free Enterprise

America got the message about the power of free enterprise at its first permanent English colony at Jamestown. For the first two years of the colony's existence, it was a mini socialist state. The colony had a common garden that everyone was supposed to work and eat from. During the first two winters, nearly half of the colonists died of starvation. The third year everyone was given their own plot of land to grow their own food, and no one ever starved again in Jamestown.

Idealists believe that we should all work harder for the common good, and just about everyone will "amen" this, but less than 1% will actually do it. Success is built on knowing the way things are, not just the way we think they should be. Just the initiative created by the basic biblical truth that if you want to eat you must work will get virtually everyone doing something productive. Wherever the entitlement mentality has taken root, there is not only a plunge in human productivity, but also the subsequent darkening of the human soul that causes the worst social problems. It is a simple equation—to the degree that you remove personal initiative, you reduce productivity and responsibility.

To a large degree, it was the lack of an entitlement mentality that enabled America to reach unprecedented economic heights. To the degree that the entitlement mentality has crept in, there has been an increasing struggle to make progress.

This is not to imply that we should not care for the less fortunate, but it is how we care for them that will determine if we have indeed helped them or doomed them—and maybe the rest of us.

Thomas Jefferson said that the Republic could not last once the people learned they could vote for those who would distribute to them the resources in the national treasury. This has happened over the last three quarters of a century. The weight of this anchor has become steadily heavier, and if not corrected, it will soon grind America's progress to a halt leading to increasing poverty.

It is not too late to reverse this trend. Remember that only a few passionate people can turn the whole national tide, and we are seeing this passion rise in America again. Even so, we are now fighting for our national survival. The wealth of the treasury has been distributed and is now gone. Instead of adjusting our policies as responsibility should dictate, we're pretending we can just print more money and have more. Again, there is a difference between wealth and currency, and we are about to learn this the hard way if we do not change our course very soon.

CHAPTER SIX
VISIONARY REGULATION

Even though some of worst crises America is now facing are the result of a lack of oversight and good regulation in sectors, the answer to our present economic crisis is not more regulation. Overregulation was actually a factor that led to the crises. Those who should have been watching for the impending dangers were too tied up majoring on minors. We do not need more regulation—we need the right regulations, properly enforced. We can manage the economy much better, and be much safer, with a small fraction of the regulations we now have.

It has been years since the crash of 2008, and to date, some of the most basic causes of that crisis have still not been corrected, or even addressed. More laws have been passed, and new regulations have been implemented, with many of these actually being counterproductive and weakening us further. These did not help us get out of the ditch, to use President Obama's metaphor, but have made it harder to get out. Even so, the vehicle itself, the core of the American economy, is still in good shape, and once we get the car out of the ditch, it will run just fine.

The Flight Plan

Managing the economy is a lot like flying an airplane. You start planning your flight by knowing where you want to go. Then you figure distances and the weather en route and at the destination.

You want to compute the fuel needed and the altitudes for avoiding such things as turbulence and icing. You determine the best possible tailwinds or how to avoid the worst headwinds. Great flights start with thorough planning, while being prepared for the unexpected conditions you did not plan for. Most flight training is actually spent on how to deal with emergencies or unexpected conditions. A good pilot will be ready for anything that might happen.

This is why U.S. Airways pilot Captain Sullenberger, who so skillfully landed his plane in the Hudson River after bird strikes shut down both of his engines, was being honest when he said he just did what any other pilot would have done in that situation. Every airline pilot has practiced power off landings over and over, and most probably would have done it just as well. Of course, the main factor is keeping your cool, following the procedures under the stress of an emergency. No one really knows how they will do in an emergency until they actually have to do it, which is why all other airline pilots also applauded the crew for their Hudson River landing.

One factor that you learn as a pilot that is pertinent to our present economic situation is that in turbulence you have to be proactive and take firm control of the airplane. However, over-control is one of the most dangerous things you can do. Over-control can lead to overstressing the airframe, which could actually cause the plane to break up. For example, a 60-degree bank doubles the stress on a plane's airframe. Doing this when the plane is in turbulence and is already taking it close to the maximum stress it can handle can be catastrophic. The same is true in an economy with economic turbulence. We need firm, decisive leadership, but one of the worst threats at this time is over-control or overreaction to the problems.

From the last days of the Bush Administration until now there has been a lot of scary overreaction to the crises. Even if we make it through this storm without breaking up, there has been some serious damage done that will need repair.

The Derivatives Threat

Some of the most dangerous threats now facing America have still not been openly discussed at this time. These are issues that need regulation, but instead the attention has been given to regulating things that are not the main threat and may not even be problems at all. While we're on this theme of discussing some of our great problems, let's start with one of the big ones-—derivatives.

A derivative is a financial instrument like "futures" that has a value based on the expected future price of the asset to which it is linked, or what is called the "underlying asset." These may look like instruments just for speculation, but there is a bit more to it than that. To understand it better, we'll look at an exaggerated example that can also show the potential impact of futures trading in general.

Futures are options you can purchase at a fraction of the price of the underlying asset because you are not actually buying the asset, but the right to buy it at a certain time at a certain price. For example, if you think gasoline is going up, you may want to buy options to purchase gasoline at a certain price, and if it goes up beyond the price you set, your options become more valuable to that degree.

For our example we will use arbitrary round numbers. Let's say that gasoline is now $2.50 a gallon wholesale. You buy the options to purchase 100,000 gallons at $2.60 a gallon in 90 days. These were 100 options to purchase 1,000 gallons each that cost $1.00 for each option, or $100.00 for all of them. They were this cheap because at the time they were buying the asset at more than it was currently selling for. Then the wholesale price of gas jumps to $3.00 per gallon, or $.40 more per gallon than you can buy it for with your options. The value of your options could then jump to about $40,000 to reflect the jump in gasoline prices. Unless you were a gasoline retailer seeking to actually buy the underlying asset, you would then sell this option and take your winnings.

This is an exaggerated example, though you can actually have this kind of windfall with options. Even if the price moves far less,

47

but in the direction you were betting on, you can make huge profits with options trading. Of course, you can also lose your principal investment, but it is still a rather small risk compared to what you can make. This is the problem—options trading can actually affect the markets and drive the value of the underlying asset up or down. Just a few speculators can drive prices up on things like gasoline that can have a devastating impact on the whole world's economy. This is, by the way, a reason why the prices we pay at the pump can sometimes make large jumps up or down that do not seem to otherwise make much sense.

Of course, some large companies, or investors, can pour in enough to have a major impact on the markets all by themselves. It is understandable that a major oil company might want to do this to drive up the value of its product, which is why you have to have regulations that protect the markets from this type of manipulation. Some speculators, like George Soros, have been accused of crashing the currencies of whole nations by using options. Some accuse him of trying to do this with the U.S. dollar because of statements he's made to this effect.

Should speculators have this kind of power to manipulate markets with options? It is understandable that companies, institutions, or even governments that actually use the underlying asset should be able to invest in futures markets. For example, an airline can use futures contracts to know what their fuel costs will be for certain future periods, which can help them control their operating costs and set ticket prices. That is legitimate, but why should these markets be open to those who are just speculators, who can leverage their investments in a way that can, in the case of gasoline, impact the whole world's economy? One solution—limit derivatives trading to those who have a legitimate interest in the market other than speculation.

One popular derivative of late was created by bundling together mortgages. Some blame the sub-prime crisis on speculators in this market. The sub-prime crisis had deeper roots than this, but these mortgage-backed derivatives did play a part in what caused a lot of pain for virtually the entire world. I will discuss the mortgage-backed derivatives in much more depth in Chapter Eleven. Some believe just the derivatives markets alone have grown to the size where they threaten the entire world's economy.

The present estimated value of derivatives in world markets has ranged from $620 to $1,000 trillion dollars. Now consider that the value of everything in the world is estimated to be between $350 and $550 trillion dollars. How could derivatives that are based on the underlying value of just a fraction of the material resources of the world be so much higher than the value of everything in the world? This can indicate a bubble, or prices that have been inflated by speculation and therefore don't have the foundational strength for sustainability. The bursting of such bubbles has caused the greatest shakeups in world markets since the 1600s. Speculators driving markets far away from their true values is one of the greatest dangers to legitimate capitalism, which is using capital to create real wealth.

The questions about derivatives lead to other obvious questions, such as the following: What is the real value of these derivatives that are such a popular investment for some of our top banks and financial institutions? The pressure put on banks to make so many sub-prime loans drove them to using derivatives as a hedge against expected losses from them. That was bad, but now we have to ask how many banks and financial institutions are using these derivatives as collateral or as assets on their books? If they are, you have to determine the true value of them to determine what these banks are really worth.

For banks and financial institutions to use derivatives to hedge against loss is one thing, but when they enter this market as speculators, it is another matter, and a very serious one. Many believe this is the main factor that began the 2008 collapse that almost crashed the entire world's markets and still has us at the edge of the cliff.

This is a necessary over-simplification of the derivatives issue, but this is still hanging over the world economy like Damocles' sword. There is a way out, and we cannot delay much longer in taking it. Again, a possible solution is to limit speculators who cause unsustainable bubbles in prices that result in devastating consequences. We need to recognize when this is happening and step in with the necessary controls, but not over-control in ways that can also bend and distort markets.

The 800-pound Gorilla

The 800-pound gorilla metaphor is for something so huge that everyone pretends it is just not there. That is what world debt is, and this is presently the biggest world threatening crisis. Some have estimated that world debt now exceeds the estimated value of everything in the world. When the obligations of governments for entitlements are thrown on top of this, we unquestionably have obligations that far outweigh our present assets. We still have time to escape this potential doom, but we don't have time to waste.

We can also be encouraged that nations have been in this type of crisis before and emerged from them. Germany and Japan were probably the most devastated nations in history after World War II. In an amazingly short time, they were again two of the most powerful nations in the world economically. The Marshall Plan helped, but there was far more to their recoveries than this, and the recovery of the other nations devastated by that war. Even so, we don't have to go through devastation, and it would be much better not to.

We've briefly addressed some major issues we need to face if we are going to get out of our present jeopardy, much less prevail in the modern world. What we will address in the next chapter will help provide an even more clear understanding of the times and the issues we still need to face. These factors are not complicated and will help us see more and more clearly where we are and where we need to go.

CHAPTER SEVEN
LIBERTY OR DEATH

Amerida remains the greatest hope in the world for those who seek freedom. Freedom is also America's only hope. Freedom is the core value of America, and it cannot be taken without destroying the essence of what America is. Many believe any people will trade freedom for security when threatened, and though some certainly will, not all will, and it is not likely that America will.

There has never been another nation in history like America. What other combatant has ever defeated its enemies in terrible and costly wars, and instead of dominating and plundering their subdued foe, have helped them rebuild and then set them free? Freedom is a core value of America that it has remained faithful to like no other nation in history.

Fuel for Progress

America is not actually a capitalist nation, but it is a nation where anyone can be a capitalist and is free to prosper from investments. As stated, there is a difference between capitalism and free enterprise, and the real basis of America is free enterprise. Great capitalists have started and prospered in America because of the opportunity they had with free enterprise. Most venture capitalists are those who have won at free enterprise and are devoted to helping other start-ups do the same. Of course, they want and deserve a reward for their risk, but capitalism helps make free enterprise possible. Both are the children of freedom, and the prosperity and strength of modern civilization have been built on them.

Business is not just a game, but for the sake of understanding it, let's consider it one. Would you want to play a game where the more you win, the more the referee comes and takes away your winnings? This is what "taxing the rich" above others actually does, and it destroys both free enterprise and undercuts basic economic initiative.

This mentality of penalizing people more for winning, which is done usually at great risk and a lot of very hard work, not only discourages others from playing the game, but it has started driving some of the best and brightest business minds in the world to other countries. Those minds are the wealth of America more than their dollars in the banks, which they are also taking with them.

At this writing, America has the second highest corporate tax rate in the world. Then our media and government criticize them for moving to other countries. Most would much rather stay in America, but they cannot continue to compete in the world market with such a heavy tax burden. Most of these are happy to pay their fair share, but not many will keep playing the game here with much devotion if we promise to take more from them the more they win. This is not only unfair, but then they get treated with scorn and disgust, which has been the recent government attitude toward its own most successful citizens. This does not help our future.

On top of this attitude by the government toward our most successful citizens, other factors are driving some of the great American companies and business leaders to other countries. The corporate taxes in America are becoming intolerable, but the overregulation is even worse. Unnecessary and counterproductive regulations are so binding our companies, and in some cases costing them more than the taxes, that they simply can no longer operate profitably in America. Many have no choice but to move to a country more favorable to business if they are going to survive.

Some may be moving just because they want to be in a place where they are honored and appreciated for their hard work. If you have not owned a business, it is not possible to understand the pressures that come with it. Most small business owners work 12 to 16 hours a day, 7 days a week. Many are risking everything they have to start and build their business, and the odds of success are not good. About 75% of all startup businesses fail in the first year. Only about 10% make it for more than two years. Those who have become established have run a most challenging gauntlet, and then to be threatened and made to pay more taxes than others by your government if you become successful is not a good way for any government to encourage business.

Many decry the huge salaries of corporate executives, and some may be exorbitant, but almost no one talks about how the average longevity of a corporate CEO is just eighteen months. The pressure cooker at the top position in almost any organization can be more than anyone can imagine who has not been there. Even then most make far less than someone can make playing professional sports. Some of these are true heroes who turn companies around and save multitudes of jobs, not to mention the impact they can have on our national economy.

No doubt some corporate executives are driven by greed, and some bad people who have a disregard for rules and others will end up hurting many. However, these are a small percentage of our business leaders, and most are heroes who deserve our thanks, not our scorn. Those who make such an impact in Britain get knighted. We need to have some kind of major national award for those who do well in our country. Those who succeed in America do benefit us all. Those who call this "trickle down economics" are only revealing a profound lack of understanding basic economics.

Freedom Restraints

Presently, one of our biggest threats to future American economic leadership is overregulation. As stated, this is becoming more costly to many businesses in America than taxes. Even if it just takes mindshare for paperwork that could be used to innovate or explore new markets, this can be crippling to our economic progress. Of course, some regulation is necessary, but one of the most helpful things we could do to help move our economy along is to get rid of the foolish, unnecessary regulations.

Good regulations are like tracks for a train. If a train had its own mind, it might think it would be freer without the tracks that keep it from wandering across the meadows and fields. However, it is the tracks that enable it to be what it was created to be so that it can go forward with all of its strength. The train may be more "free" if it could jump the tracks, but it would quickly get bogged down and unable to move. Necessary regulations are like the tracks that help keep the train free to do what it was created to do.

Many regulations imposed by government are necessary, but many can look good and be easy enough to comply with, but when added together with all of the other good-and-easy-to-comply-with regulations, they become a huge weight on an industry or our whole economy. This is speculation because I do not have the personal resources to do the research, but if the amount of time spent on unnecessary regulations in America were added up over a year, I am quite sure that if that time was spent on productivity instead, we would easily balance our Federal budget even with the $2 trillion dollars plus debt that they claim is only $1.5 trillion.

We need to get regulations down to what is essential and develop a mentality that resists any regulations until they are proven necessary, not have the present mentality that thinks more regulations are good.

Butterflies and Hurricanes

It has been said that a butterfly flapping its wings in Asia can cause a hurricane in another part of the world. This is an exaggeration, but a small action can have major consequences in far away and unexpected ways as any major manufacturer or engineer knows. One simple change on one station on an assembly line that only takes a few seconds can cost millions or even more to the costs of the plant. If you can only see your own station, this may not make sense, but if you see all of the consequences it can have down the line, and then up the line, most would be amazed.

Likewise, a policy or procedure can have major and devastating unforeseen consequences throughout an industry and affect every American's cost of living. Virtually everything we do now is part of a process where one little change almost anywhere in it can have huge and unforeseen consequences by the end of the process. This is why change must be managed by someone who understands and has oversight of the entire process.

A few years ago, we purchased the largest hotel in our state with more than five hundred rooms. Our hospitality department found a little piece of furniture to put in each room that they thought would be a nice touch. They only cost about $50 each, but multiplied by 500, made them cost $25,000. Then I asked how much time this would add to cleaning each room by dusting it and having to move around it. If it adds just five minutes a room, over a year it could cost us enough to hire another worker in hospitality. Carrying it out further, I had to decide if this nice little touch was worth half a million dollars over 10 years. On the surface the decision just looked like a small thing, but in the big picture it was a major decision.

The government often looks at another regulation or report required as only taking a few minutes each, but it can cost the country millions, and possibly even billions a year when added up. Couldn't that money be spent better somewhere else, or on someone else, especially when no one is likely to ever read that report anyway? Sure, the report might come in handy somewhere and sometime in a special situation, but for what we're paying for this, is it worth that convenience?

Not only that, if we really care about the environment, why isn't someone screaming about the millions of trees that have to die every year to make the paper for this foolishness?

In passing laws, our government has proven to be shortsighted and short of common sense. It might not be so out of touch if our representatives were citizen representatives as was initially planned, with them having to go home and live with their own laws.

We need lawyers for functioning in the modern world, but we only need a fraction of the number we have now. One reason why the economies of India and China are doing so well while ours is floundering is because both of those nations produce about eight engineers for every lawyer. We are producing eight lawyers for every engineer. The pathway to power in China, India, and the other emerging superpower economies is through engineering, not the legal profession. Their leaders, who are mostly from engineering backgrounds, approach both problems and opportunities like engineers, not lawyers. An engineer is trained to follow the consequences of every action to its conclusion. Few politicians, who are mostly lawyers, seem to understand this concept.

I read the first healthcare reform bill proposed, HR 3200 and tried to see it from a manager's or engineer's perspective. I will be kind and say it was shocking. I could not believe the madness that someone actually put on paper. What has been unpackaged in this bill has been no less shocking. That our representatives would ram something like this down the throats of the American people without even reading, much less studying and considering the consequences of what they were doing, has to be one of the worst betrayals of the trust given to our representatives in history.

With just a little common sense we know the government will manage our healthcare like they manage everything else, and that is a very frightening prospect. Only the most dim could read that bill and not see that rationing is inevitable. Our healthcare costs are going to either multiply fast or the quality and quantity of what is available is going to drop correspondingly fast. It is likely that our healthcare system is doomed to be but a shell of what it has been—the best in the world.

If the most brilliant minds in the world were going to do what our government is going to try to do, they would have taken months, if not years, just to plan how to do it. What our government slapped together in a few days, done by those who don't know what they're doing anyway, especially not in such a technical field as healthcare, is madness. And it is going to cost a lot more than gazillions of dollars—it is going to cost many lives. A less gracious people would have considered something like this being done to it as criminal, if not treason.

The Financial Reform Act will also have some dire consequences. I was told that the financial reform legislation may not have anything in it about small banks, but what it has in it ensures that local banks in America are doomed. If this is true, then it could ultimately kill free enterprise in America because the small community banks are the lifeblood of small start-up businesses. I talked to a small banker about it, and he was already planning to close his bank because so many more additional reports were being required of him that he estimated it would cost him an additional several hundred thousand dollars a year more, and he just could not afford it. Bigger banks could more easily absorb this extra burden, but it will wipe out many small ones, or weaken them further, when the point is supposed to be to strengthen our banking system.

Some believe that the Financial Reform Act was intended to wipe out small community banks by the Administration because they thought the banks were too independent and unmanageable. Perhaps. But even if they are independent and hard to oversee, do they need more oversight? None of our present financial crises were caused by small banks, so why would we want to shut them down? Even if we give the Administration the benefit of the doubt that this was not intentional, it will still be the consequence. A drunk driver may not have wanted to hurt anyone, but their victims are dead nonetheless. At best, our government is acting like a drunk driver now, and at worst, it is intentionally unraveling the very fabric that made America the strongest and most prosperous nation in history.

The Connect

I share the basic premise of conservatives that those who are closest to the issues are those who should have most of the authority to make the laws and regulations that affect them. Some things only our Federal government can do of course, but even those should be managed well. The rest should be done either by the states or cities and counties, whichever has the best connection to the issues. The Constitution actually mandates that all authority not specifically given to the Federal government remains the authority of the states.

Since the Civil War just about everyone is afraid to even use the term "states' rights" because this argument was used to defend slavery. The result has been the states simply caving in and abdicating much, if not most, of their authority to the Federal government. The consequences of this have almost all been bad, and some have been catastrophic. The Founding Fathers got it right, and the Constitution is right.

Local government should have most of the authority over local issues. Certainly the local governments would be much more in touch with the needs and possible problems with local banks, but the Federal government has seized this authority by using the FDIC, insurance that every bank must now have. By destroying the local community banks in America, our Federal government just took a much stronger grip over our entire economy. Having the evidence that we do about how the government runs everything under its control, we know the Federal government's grip cannot help but to have terrible consequences for American business if not reversed.

Even more important than the certain economic upheaval is how the Federal government is taking away our basic freedoms. Soon it will have virtual control over how much life, liberty, and pursuit of happiness we can have. The reverse is what our Constitution mandates—that we the people should decide how much our government has. We can still determine this, and the movements now arising in America are a great encouragement that the people of America have been pushed too far. They are going to take back their country and bring their government back under submission to the people.

The ultimate objective is to find the balance between what needs to be the responsibility of our central government and what needs to remain the responsibility and the authority of our local governments who are closer to most of the day-to-day, real-life issues of the local people. Because we are all connected together as one nation, we also need to keep in mind that some laws passed on a local basis could have national implications. So at what point is it significant enough to make a Federal law? A lawyer may tend to say we need a law to determine this, but in most cases we do not need a law for that; however, a leader will tend to lead in each situation. Some things need room to develop to see if the fruit is good or bad, and if it is bad, we need to determine whether it is bad enough to yoke the entire nation with another law to regulate it.

Legal or Right

It is a remarkable accomplishment and testimony that our economy has done as well as it has with the opposition it has from the world markets and from our own government. One thing is certain—our economy is the strongest in the world, which is evidenced by how it still functions despite all of the obstacles and burdens it is now carrying. It has an amazing resilience to continually get knocked down and still get up and press on. If it dies, it will not be from natural causes; nor will it be defeated by the world markets. Rather, it will have been murdered by our own government.

There is still time to set our people and our economy free to be all that they can be. As covered, some of the most important steps are to ensure that necessary regulations are in place, remove unnecessary regulations, and make our economic policies friends and allies of the business community instead of the adversaries they too often are now. This must include a simplified tax code and regulations written in plain, clear English, not legalese. This would reduce many regulations to 10% of their present size or less, freeing government workers who enforce them and those who must comply with them of countless hours of wasted time and energy. They would also be freed from a huge amount of confusion in trying to understand what some of the regulations actually mean.

Years ago a test was done on the IRS "Help Line," and it was found that IRS agents answered wrong to the most commonly asked questions 40% of the time. I don't blame the IRS for this, rather the people who write the regulations and policies. That the IRS could understand its own regulations 60% of the time is laudable.

We need only the necessary regulations, and they should be written so that those who must comply with them can quickly and easily understand them. Legalese is the language of Babylon, which means "confusion." Most contracts can say everything needed and say everything better in 10% of the pages most of them now are. The main reason we have legalese can be summed up in two words—billable hours.

Years ago I began demanding that any contract I sign be a fraction of the size of what was first presented to me, and that it be written in plain English. I got contracts that first came with more than twenty pages down to three or four. I always ask if anything was left out, and the answer is always "no." I've also watched the way some lawyers get this, and they seem as if they are like a bird let out of a cage. Nobody is more bored and tortured than they are by having to read that madness every day.

We are not only dependent on lawyers to write contracts, but then we need others to read them who can understand the language. This way the work we have to pay for is doubled. There is nothing magical about a contract. The terms should be stated as plainly, clearly, and succinctly as possible. This is another way that we, the people, can take control of our own lives—don't sign anything you cannot read and understand yourself.

For proof of how silly these contracts are, and actually counter-productive, in just the last couple of decades mortgage contracts went from just a couple of pages to a pile impossible for someone to read at a closing. Did all of this help make mortgages safer? What has most of the crisis been about the last few years?

We can no longer tolerate the amount of time and expense going into reading and trying to understand contracts and regulations. With all the lawsuits we hear about, we may think we need an army of lawyers. We don't. We will discuss this in a bit more detail later.

Sound the Alarm!

We are facing a number of crises at this time, each of which could be our doom as a Republic. At this writing the potential economic meltdown is the most desperate of these crises. The more the government claims that we are climbing out of this, the more suspect we should be of its actual condition. It's tragic that we can no longer trust our government to tell us the truth, but that is a fact, which only the most dull and naïve do not understand.

Without question, integrity must be restored, but there is also another way we can get out of the ditch we're still stuck in. We must embrace "American exceptionalism." This may sound like typical American pride, but it is not. There are ways that America is an exception to every other nation on earth, and this has been a basis of our extraordinary prosperity and our most basic strengths. We must return to our American roots.

Another basic answer to our present situation is to simplify. Some claim that our economy is now so complicated that the answers for correcting it are not going to be simple. However, the reverse is true. Just consider that many of our most devastating problems have come with overly complex economic vehicles. We don't need them. Complexities are often imposed to hide things that some do not want others to see.

Simplification itself can be a powerful jumpstart to a stalled economy. Just a few steps could not only set it on a course for stable and enduring economic health, but also help to resolve some of the other crises that are interconnected to it.

As the saying goes, "If you do not change your direction, you will end up where you are headed." Where we are now headed is a breakdown of the whole system. That will lead to either anarchy or totalitarian control—or, what is more likely, anarchy followed by totalitarian control. That may sound dramatic, but we are precariously close to this scenario now.

Our leaders are boasting that we have now "pulled away from the edge" of our economic crisis, but some of the most experienced and greatest minds in the world see something else. Even so, out of this crisis we can emerge stronger and more stable than ever if we take action to change course soon. The collapse of our economy is not necessary, and neither is our decline. We may be lingering dangerously close to the edge, but with so many more growing in understanding, there is growing hope for our future.

CHAPTER EIGHT

A SUPERSIZED ANSWER

Ronald Reagan said, "Government is not a solution to our problem, government is the problem." This is still true. Government could indeed be part of the solution, but major changes must be made in government first. It is not just too big and consuming too much of the wealth and resources of the nation; it is also dysfunctional and incompetent. It is not likely to be able to pull our economy out of the quagmire it's now in because we have to be standing on solid ground before we can pull someone else out of the quicksand, and our government is in far worse shape than the economy.

Every level of government can be reduced in size. Each level needs to be reengineered and strengthened in the right way to start again fulfilling its purpose to serve the people, not consume the resources of the people. A cancer forms when cells start consuming selfishly without regard for the rest of the body. The government in America has cancer. We must do radical surgery to remove the tumors, or we will not live much longer as a nation.

There is no reason why the government cannot be run with the same efficiency and effectiveness with which any business is run. The key to making this happen is accountability. A business cannot just tax its customers; it has to have a marketable product that people want, and then it has to be run with efficiency to survive and then prosper. The government's lack of accountability when it needs more money by raising taxes, borrowing it, or even printing more money, has led to unprecedented irresponsibility in both efficiency and quality control in government. More controls and safeguards are needed to keep the government in check than are needed for the private sector.

More are starting to believe the United States will not survive much longer without a Constitutional Amendment that requires our Federal government to live on a balanced budget. This would be with the exception of war or a declared economic emergency that is clearly defined. Whether this is required for our survival can be debated, but without question, it is needed to rein in the nightmarish foolishness in fiscal irresponsibility our government has demonstrated to date.

Our entire Federal budget just recently hit $1 trillion dollars, and then shot so far past it that we are now close to paying $1 trillion dollars a year just in interest on our debt. Our debt is still rising faster than has ever been seen in history, and at this writing, virtually nothing has been done to cut spending! This obviously cannot be sustained for long. We got here because of a lack of leadership, and nothing is being done about it because of a lack of leadership. We will need extraordinary leadership to turn this around.

Presently, there is probably not a more poorly run entity on the planet than the Federal government. It should be the opposite. Our government is the sacred trust of the people, and the people deserve much better than we have been getting. Government should have an even higher standard of efficiency and effectiveness than business, but this is not going to happen until the people demand it and hold it accountable. The ones we have trusted our resources to have been bad stewards, and they must be fired. The elections of 2010 were a start, but it is far from the radical transformation in government that we must have.

With sound management, our U.S. government could be 20% of its present size while accomplishing much more than it does now.

That should be our goal, and it is achievable. It cannot be done overnight, but it could easily be done within 10 years. To the leaders who say this is not possible, we need to say that it is not possible with them in office, so we will replace them.

With our government the right size for its responsibility, literally 20% of its present size, we would not have deficits, could easily handle the entitlements promised, and the economy of America would have trillions of dollars more flowing to it every year. Think of the positive impact this one thing could have. We can do this. We have to do this. It will take the public rising up and demanding it and not accepting a halfway job. That is beginning to happen.

For the People

The U.S. government was created to serve the people, not to be served by them. It was created to protect our wealth and resources, not consume them. Government workers, from the President down, were to be public servants, not the privileged class they have set themselves up to be. The imperial nature and attitude that our government has evolved into must be changed. We must resolve to never again elect professional politicians, and determine it is one species we will make extinct in our country. We, the people, must resolve that every elected office in government should be filled with leaders and managers who have a mission and know how to accomplish it.

The Founding Fathers warned about such a class of people who have come to dominate elected offices in America—the professional politicians whom they said would be the doom of the Republic. This is coming true. We need a second American Revolution to return us to the government intended by the first one.

The One-headed Monster

If you could picture the present state of our government as a human body, it would be about 80% head with a tiny little body attached. The head, government bureaucracy, needs to be shrunk down until it is again rightly proportioned to the rest of the body. If you wonder how the country could function if we did this, it can be summed up in one word—better!

For a century, our elected officials have been flailing at the branches of government inefficiency and waste, but the ax must be put to the root of the tree. Radical change is needed in the structure of government from every bureau through every elected position. We need to return to the original structure of the Republic established by the Founding Fathers. They got it right.

Some might protest that this is not possible in the modern world, but in fact, it would work even better in the modern world with all of the automation and computerization we now have. The principles of government that were the foundation of our Republic had nothing to do with whether we were mostly an agrarian or industrial society as many constitutional adversaries claim, but it had to do with controlling flawed human character, especially the kind that has taken over our government!

Turning the Ship of State

We should never want to silence protest, or challenges, because these only help to sharpen our ideas and our leaders. However, we must replace the negative, problem-oriented people now entrenched in the leadership of our government with positive, solution-oriented people. Regardless of what our politicians say, our government now believes that we the people exist for it, instead of it existing for us. This has to change, and change now.

The ship of state is very large, and an aircraft carrier cannot be turned like a speedboat. The Federal government got to the present state of inefficiency and ineffectiveness in over more than a century, so it is not reasonable to think that it can be corrected overnight. Even so, it can be done in 10 years and maybe less. The size of our government could easily be cut by 10% a year while dramatically improving the services it provides. In just 5 years, the government would be approaching half its present size, and in just a few more it would be at the right size.

At this writing, Britain is cutting its budget across the board by 20%. If we wait much longer, we will have to speed up the cuts too, maybe even lopping off more than 20% at first. The most humane and efficient way to accomplish all that we're discussing here is to do it as slowly as possible. This will be fast enough to create and keep the momentum going, but also slow enough to allow people to make the necessary adjustments in their lives and will allow the government to implement more efficient procedures.

Continuous Growth

Government-centric people protest that cutting government is cutting jobs, and this will have a negative impact on the economy, but as with much of the present mentality, the reverse is true. Cutting the size of government will have the biggest positive impact on our economy of possibly anything ever. Again, it would release over $1 trillion more dollars a year to flow through the economy that is now going into the black hole of government mismanagement. The freeing up of these resources would be like providing unlimited fuel to our economic engine and would make everything on our list at the beginning of this book easily achievable.

We must demand leadership that will give no quarter to government waste and inefficiency, knowing that this is the people's money and resources that are being devoured. We have a sacred trust not to do this or to ever let this happen again. It does take bold new thinking just to see it, and it will take a bold new breed of leadership to make it happen. We are in our present state because of a lack of leadership, and we will not get to where we need to go without a bold new breed of leadership.

If you are asking why the best minds in our country have not thought about all of this before, I would counter that they have, but the best minds in our country are not in government. The best and the brightest are drawn to just about any other field than government because the government's whole culture at this time is foreign to true leadership. One of our great challenges is to get some of the best and the brightest engaged in government again. It will be a sacrifice for them, but that is the way our government was designed—to be led by true public servants who do it as service, not a profession.

All Hands on Deck

I was stationed at a land base for a year when I was in the Navy. Because everyone there had to be a part of the ground defense force, we all had to go through basic infantry training with the Marines. If the base was attacked, we all had to fight the attack regardless of what our job was. We are in such a situation now—our whole way of life is under assault from virtually every direction and we all must mobilize to defeat it.

Later, when I was on an aircraft carrier, even though I was in aviation, if there was a fire or battle damage, everyone was trained to be part of the damage control team. If there was a hole in the ship, everyone was focused on getting that hole fixed, or none of us would have a job, or maybe even a life. We are in that kind of emergency now. At least for a time, we must focus on getting the hole in the ship fixed. When repaired, the ship will be capable of going much farther, but if we do not address the crisis at hand, we will sink very soon. Let's get her fixed, and then get going again. We still have much to accomplish as a nation.

CHAPTER NINE
IT'S YOUR MONEY

True value cannot be measured by how much money people have, but we can learn a great deal about them by how they use or manage what they have. This was so important to Jesus that He said we could not be trusted with the **"true riches" (see Luke 16:11)** if we did not learn how to handle earthly riches. It has also been estimated that between one-third and one-half of the biblical teachings on righteousness have to do with stewardship, that is, how we manage the resources we are trusted with.

Effectively and efficiently managing our resources should also be basic criteria for judging government. If it is inefficient, it is wasting the people's resources. To write about government waste and inefficiency is certainly a "target-rich environment." There seems to be unlimited examples of government mismanagement on a level that would have a private citizen committed for insanity by doing the same with their resources. We are the insane ones if we let it continue. Thankfully, the American people are demanding change.

It is encouraging to see how the American people are not letting go some very important questions like what happened to the first $350 billion in TARP funds? Why can't our government tell us where that much money went? Who did the accounting for it? The word "accounting" comes from "accountability." Who let so much of our money just disappear?

Our government is presently demonstrating a basic and maybe unprecedented lack of accountability. That is bad, but it is then treating the American people with contempt as if we are too slow or simple to understand. If we had done the same things in business that our government has been doing, we would be in jail. Why does the government, which is charged with handling so much more, not have even higher standards of accountability than the private sector?

Obviously very little of the TARP funds or the stimulus money, over $1 trillion dollars altogether, went to where we were told it was going. If it did, it had virtually none of the expected results. We were told that if this money was not spent, the unemployment rate could even surpass 8%, so the American public was frightened into going along with it. Then the unemployment rate raced well past the then-terrifying 8% to nearly 10%, and at this writing, has been there for 2 years.

Remember the website www.Recovery.gov? Investigators followed up on the information provided on this White House-managed site and could not verify but a small percentage of the jobs supposedly created or saved by the stimulus money. What the investigators were able to verify was that most of data provided on this website had been wildly exaggerated. Many of the places that jobs were supposedly created or saved did not even exist. Even congressional districts referred to on this site did not exist. It appeared that someone was just throwing up numbers arbitrarily.

Not only is this kind of blatant lying to the American people further shattering the trust of the people for their government, but what would happen to a company that skewed its corporate report? The leaders of that company would go to prison for a long time. Why is our government allowed to get away with this kind of lying to the American people? Why is it a crime to lie to the government but it is not a crime when the government lies to the American people?

Stuck in the Mud

President Obama has often used the metaphor of a car run into a ditch to describe what has happened to our economy. It is a good analogy to use. A car can have 300-horsepower and exert every bit of it but still not be going anywhere if it is stuck in the sand. That would be a good picture of our U.S. economy. The government keeps hitting the accelerator, pouring the gas to it, and the engine is revving, but we're not going anywhere. Why?

The government first put the pedal to the metal by throwing $350 billion dollars at it, and it did not move. It threw another $350 billion right after that—nothing. Since then, we have thrown hundreds of billions more, but in the President's own words, we are still stuck. So what was his Administration's answer to this dilemma? At first it was another stimulus—throw more money at it! The population made it clear this would not be tolerated and so the government was restrained, but it was shocking enough that this would even be proposed.

The reason our economy is still in the ditch is simple—nothing is wrong with the car or its engine; we simply are not getting any traction. Pouring more gas in the tank or putting the pedal to the metal again is not going to help. We need to put something under the tires so it can get traction. Corporations are flush with cash right now—they just won't spend it. So how do we get traction?

The government actually has been using the present economic crisis to make radical changes to the engine, and indeed the entire car, and they are not running as well now as when it went into the ditch. The mechanics working on it simply don't know what they're doing. This can be fixed, but just the foolishness of it scared many away from investing or expanding their business. What is needed is someone at the wheel who can drive. The car is not the problem. It got off track because of the way it was driven. Why are we trying to repair the car that runs fine instead of addressing the real problem? We need someone to drive it who knows what they're doing, so we can get it back on the road.

The basic economic engine of the U.S. is very strong and resilient. It has been able to inch forward even while it was stuck in the ditch. If the billions in TARP money was used for what they told the American people it would be used for, to buy up the toxic debt to get it off of bank balance sheets so they would be free to start lending again, we could be out of the ditch and humming along again. Instead, we have dug an even bigger hole because the money was just thrown to banks and financial institutions without even giving them guidelines about how it was to be used. This is another basic management failure by our government as well as a lack of accountability. So why should we trust them?

Remember Einstein's definition of insanity—do the same thing over and over, expecting different results? We are the ones who are insane if we keep trusting those who are now running our government. We must have new leadership. This is more than just electing different people to Congress, or as our President—we need a leadership throughout government that has a radically different mentality about government and how it should be run.

Like the TARP program, the near trillion dollars in stimulus money ($787 billion) was probably the most poorly managed government program yet, and the proof is almost everywhere you turn now. The 40-page report released by the City of Los Angeles is a graphic example of how our money was spent. The headline pretty much says it all, but as you read on, it is hard to imagine this kind of thinking is going on with anyone with serious authority. This is not fiction, but a true report except for the notes in parenthesis, which are mine.

$111M in Stimulus Saved Just 55 Jobs

By William Lajeunesse
Published September 17, 2010
AFP

> *More than a year after Congress approved $800 billion in stimulus funds, the Los Angeles city controller has released a 40-page report on how the city spent its share, and the results are not living up to expectations.*

"I'm disappointed that we've only created or retained 55 jobs after receiving $111 million," said Wendy Greuel, the city's controller. "With our local unemployment rate over 12 percent we need to do a better job cutting red tape and putting Angelenos back to work."

According to the audit, the Los Angeles Department of Public Works spent $70 million in stimulus funds—in return, it created seven private sector jobs and saved seven workers from layoffs. Taxpayer cost per job: $1.5 million. (Who is doing the math for the City of Los Angeles? Isn't 70 million divided by 14 = $5,000,000 per job?) *The Los Angeles Department of Transportation created even fewer jobs per dollar, spending $40 million but netting just nine jobs. Taxpayer cost per job: $4.4 million.*

Greuel blamed the dismal numbers on several factors:

1. *Bureaucratic red tape: Four highway projects did not even go out to bid until seven months after they were authorized.*

2. *Projects that were supposed to be competitively bid in the private sector went instead went to city workers.*

3. *Stimulus money was not properly tracked within departments*

4. *Both departments could not report the jobs created and retained in a timely fashion.*

"I would say maybe in a grade, a B- in creating the jobs," Greuel told Fox News. "They have started to spend those dollars but it took seven months to get some of those contracts out. We think in the city that we should move quickly and not in the same usual bureaucratic way."

The last comment by the Los Angeles City controller may sum up this entire ridiculous but tragic scenario better than anything—she gave the city a "B minus" for the way they managed this! If there was ever a deserved "F" for a grade, an absolute FAILURE, this is it. To give this performance a "B minus" shows just how out of touch government has become from the local to the Federal. Remember, this is our money that they are throwing away like this! This is the kind of maddening inefficiency that has crippled our economy, and if it is not reversed soon it will do us in.

The government's own estimation of the cost of jobs that would be created by the stimulus was that each job would cost about $270,000. That is more than a quarter of a million dollars per job! That is the kind of mentality our government now has about how to spend our money! That was madness, and it was remarkable and disappointing that the whole country did not rise up in disgust now that it is apparent that every job created by the stimulus actually cost millions. This is untenable and unsustainable. We must have change now.

Where Do Jobs Come From?

During the Carter Administration, it was assumed that small business (defined as a business with twenty-five employees or fewer) was just a small fraction of our entire economy. One estimate was that small business made up about 5% of the entire economy. Someone decided to do a study, and to the astonishment of government, they found that small business was actually 50% of the U.S. economy, and that 70% to 80% of all new jobs were created by small business.

This has been common knowledge for more than 30 years. So why did the trillions in aid and stimulus money spent recently by our government, which was stated to be about creating jobs, not include one cent for small business where most jobs are created? The last figures revealed that of the jobs supposedly created or saved, 80% were government jobs.

It's well-known that the infrastructure of America is in serious need of rebuilding. The estimate for doing this is about $1.6 trillion. With the money squandered in just the last couple of years by bogus TARP and stimulus programs, we could already have accomplished this and more. Instead, the money seems to have just evaporated. The infrastructure is still crumbling, and the only thing expanding is our deficit. That is absolute failure of our leadership. If we keep those in office who did this to us, we will probably be the worst example in history of Einstein's definition of insanity.

Where Does Money Come From?

Asking where the money went is important, but we need to know where this money is coming from too. Of course, this is coming from us, the American people, but we also need to understand how it is being taken from the economy instead of stimulating it. This is akin to the previous incomprehensible medical practice of using leeches to bleed people in order to heal them!

Deficits are not just numbers; they represent real money that is being borrowed. It is being borrowed from those who would otherwise be investing it in the economy. The trillions of dollars in deficits that we now have are being drawn directly out of the economy, draining it of its life source. This is money that otherwise would be invested in creating marketable products, which is the only real thing that can ultimately create what everyone agrees is the top priority right now—jobs.

For those who would protest that most of our debt is now being bought by foreign governments, this is true, and it also represents another glaring failure. We have drained our people and economy of its resources so that it does not have any more to put into government bonds. We are also now having to go cap in hand before governments that do not like us at all, and this disgrace could turn into something much more sinister quickly.

The Key to Understanding

Many people sincerely do not understand why the government cannot just keep giving to people or why it cannot just print more money. This thought is not from kids who have never been taught basic economics; it is the mentality of some of our leaders! There are a few basic factors that many seem to not understand about the government—it does not make anything, and it does have anything to give to anyone that it has not taken from someone else. If it keeps taking, then those who do produce what the world needs to keep living will stop producing it. It is that simple.

Right now our government is taking from you, me, and our kids, and most likely, from generations to come. We are not receiving one thing in return for it. Of course, they are claiming that this money was used to keep the whole economy from going over the cliff, from getting much worse than it is now, but there is no evidence for that. If this were true, they could show us exactly where the money went and the impact it had. Every time they have tried to give us numbers so far, they have been caught in such lies and exaggerations that trust in our government is evaporating as fast as the money is.

Then, to confirm just how out of touch they are if any more confirmation was needed, they wonder what the Tea Party Movement is all about! Right now America is suffering under a tyranny of mismanagement that is getting much worse than the tyranny under King George.

Because no government can operate the way that ours is without eventually oppressing the people, it is easy to understand why almost every bill passed now has provisions to increase government control over the people. Americans would not put up with the tyranny of King George, and they will not put up with it from our own government either. Without radical change in the government, we are headed for another American Revolution to throw off this tyranny. The form that this revolution takes will be determined by a number of factors, but real change is coming. We simply cannot continue going in the direction we have been going much longer.

Ronald Reagan once said there were two things people should never see—the way sausage is made and the way bills are made in Congress. This is why, in spite of all of the promises of transparency by President Obama, our government has become increasingly secretive about how they are putting together the bills and what is in them. The people are finding out anyway, and each new revelation increases their alarm.

What is happening should by now be very clear to us—we are being led by people who are either trying to destroy our nation or who do not know what they are doing. Either way, the answer to getting out of the present situation is the same, and right now we don't have time to waste assigning blame. The wise thing is to blame ourselves for electing such as we have, and let this cause enough remorse to ensure that we don't allow it to happen again.

We cannot let our government ever again get so far beyond the restraints. Our government, not just the economy, must stay on the road and out of the ditch. It has drifted far from its constitutional moorings, and we must rein it back in, now.

CHAPTER TEN
BACK ON THE ROAD

The Bible has a lot to say about the path of life, or the path that leads to life. It has a ditch on either side. On one side is legalism, or the harsh, controlling pursuit of self-righteousness. On the other side is the opposite—lawlessness, or the lack of any restraints. Those who would stay on the path of life must avoid falling into either one of these ditches. Those who fall into one of the ditches usually do so because of an overreaction to the ditch on the opposite side. The same is true for America—life, prosperity, and progress are found by keeping the proper balance between too much regulation and too little regulation.

After having government dominated by lawyers for so long, we are definitely in the ditch of overregulation. Even though we are in that ditch, occasional problems do come from places where there were no regulations but should have had some. This fortifies the regulation perpetrators, but we must resist overreaction if we are going to stay on the path of life. We must also resist overreacting to regulations. Some are needed. We don't want to get out of the ditch of legalism and then fall into the ditch of lawlessness. The key is to find the balance that gives the most life, prosperity, progress, and safety.

One Step at a Time

The healthiest economy would be an asset-based economy rather than a credit-based one like we have now. This should be our ultimate national goal, but we cannot get from where we are to an asset-based economy in one leap. It's going to be a long and sometimes hard road. We must keep in mind that any job is doable if broken down into small enough steps, but our economy is so fragile at this time that it might not survive any more radical course changes until it can get back on solid ground. Before trying to get to an asset-based economy, we need to establish a healthy footing again as a credit-based economy. This starts by extending credit to only the credit-worthy and being conservative about how much is extended.

Our credit markets have been so tight since 2008 that there probably is not too much adjustment needed in this right now, unless it is to loosen it a bit until we get back on a more healthy footing. Then, without mandating or over-controlling people with regulations, we should teach basic budgeting and financial management in every school. If we set personal goals of trying to live on just 75% of our income within 5 years, and then reducing this by 5% a year, America would be a very different place within 10 years. Of course, it would be wonderful to have government as an example of financial responsibility by doing something like this too.

The U.S. economy is fixable and will heal itself to some degree without any help, but proactive leadership will be required to get it out of the ditch and rolling again with the full potential it has. The healthiest conditions for an economy are consistency, knowing what the rules are and knowing they will be evenly and fairly upheld. When there is inconsistency, or hypocrisy, it is disconcerting to everyone, but especially business.

For example, instead of holding those accountable who misused or lost the TARP money, one of the main people responsible for the TARP plan and its implementation that went so awry, Timothy Geithner, was promoted to being Secretary of the Treasury. This is considered the second most powerful office in the nation and the most crucial office for getting us out of the present crisis. This was not a confidence builder. As could be expected, instead of getting out of the ditch, the economy got mired even deeper.

Just to talk negatively about the economy is anathema because so much economic progress is based on faith in the economy, and most don't want to say anything to hurt people's faith in it. There is truth to this to a degree, but truth itself is the most solid foundation for faith. When the government is constantly caught lying to us, while trying to make the economy look better than it is, and we're told that government programs are working better than they actually are, the real faith needed for economic health is damaged far more than just by some people being negative.

The consequences for companies lying to investors or customers are long prison sentences for those responsible, and it should be because many people get hurt by such lies. However, far more people have been hurt by government lies than corporate lies. Therefore, basic to our economic recovery is the recovery of trust. This recovery of trust has to begin with an absolute, uncompromising devotion to the truth, with accountability for those in government who do not tell the truth. President Bill Clinton got impeached for not telling the truth under oath, but why should it just be a penalty for when we are under oath? Why shouldn't our government officials and leaders be responsible for telling us the truth all of the time?

Making It Through the Storm

Financial stability must begin with basic integrity—a devotion to truth and accuracy. A number of factors led to the economic crisis that started in 2008. If we understand these, it could help us avoid future crises like this, but to date, the real causes of it have still not been addressed. Until they are, we will continue to be in jeopardy of the same thing happening again. Similar economic storms are brewing and since the conditions that hit us in 2008 still exist, more such storms are likely and maybe even inevitable. Right now it is hard to tell if our leaders do not see these conditions or if they are just not going to tell us about them. Either way, until there is a leadership in place that understands and is honest with us, we need to be prepared to navigate through more storms.

The basic principles that pilots are taught for navigating through storms can be applied to helping almost any organization or government navigate through a crisis. In flight school, we were told never to get into a thunderstorm because in it you will find the most violent weather forces on earth. Then we were told, "But *when* you do get into a storm...." you can survive by following these basic procedures:

1. Stay calm

2. Take control

3. Slow down

4. Hold your heading (fly straight)

We'll now briefly look at each of these and how they might apply to us personally and nationally.

#1 Stay calm. This is critical because if we do not keep our cool in the crisis, our odds of survival decrease to that degree. Panic probably kills more people in aircraft emergencies than any other factor. In reports, this is often called "pilot error." Panic causes you to overreact and make mistakes that can be worse than the crisis. You can be an excellent pilot in all other phases, but if you're prone to panic in an emergency, you should not be a pilot. The same is true of leadership in any organization or government.

#2 Take control. The pilot, or leader, must control the situation, not let the situation control him or her. You have to be as firm as possible, and as gentle as possible at the same time, to keep from over-controlling, and therefore over-stressing the plane, or the organization. As addressed earlier, pilots spend more time training for emergencies than anything else. We train on the most common emergencies until they become second nature or automatic. To the degree that we are prepared, the easier it will be to remain calm and take the control, which will result in the right actions. As I've survived emergencies that were "worst case, worst time," I attest that regardless of how tedious and boring this training can get, it is worth it.

#3 Slow down. Every plane has what is called a "maneuvering speed," or the optimum speed for turbulence penetration. This speed is high enough above the stall speed to be safe, but also slow enough to reduce the stress on the airframe from the turbulence. Reducing to this speed requires reducing your power settings slowly so as not to overcorrect, which can also cause a stall. In an organization that gets into turbulence, we need to do the same thing—reduce our speed, but in such a way that is very controlled and does not create additional problems from overreaction.

#4 Hold your course. When you first get into a storm and severe turbulence, there is a natural tendency to just turn around and go back to where you had the smooth air. This can be a deadly mistake. A thunderhead is rarely more than a few miles wide. Going straight is the fastest way out, but there is another factor that is even more critical.

When you bank a plane to turn, you add stress to it called "G" forces, which stand for extra forces of gravity. In a 60-degree bank, you double the stress on your airframe and wings. A plane can easily handle this in smooth air, but in severe turbulence a plane can already be close to the maximum stress it can take, so if you start banking the plane to turn, you can quickly overstress the airframe. When you hear that a plane "broke up in the air," this is what happened.

For this reason, the safest thing to do in a storm is just hold your course—go straight. So in turbulence, or in turbulent times, you make only the most gentle turns possible, and only want to turn if you have to avoid something like a mountain or other obstacle.

Our economy has been in serious turbulence for a long time now, and recently, those at the controls have been jerking us into very steep turns, making radical changes in our course. The fact that the economy has not come apart yet is a testimony to just how strong it is. Even so, planes can still be damaged severely without coming apart, and maybe allow you to land, but never be safe enough to fly again without radical overhaul. Likewise, our economy may not have completely come apart from the jerking about it's been through while in the turbulence of the last few years, but it has been so damaged that it does need some major repairs to really be safe again.

When flying through a storm, you often get blown off course and need to make course corrections, but it is best to wait until you are through the storm and in clear, smooth air before making them. This is wisdom for any organization or government—when in turbulence take control, be firm but gentle, but don't try to make big course corrections while still in turbulence. Get out of the present crisis, and then you will be able to see more clearly just what course corrections are needed.

Does the Pilot Know How to Fly?

When I became a flight instructor, I learned how to recognize pilots who would freeze up in an emergency or panic and start making erratic decisions and actions. They were too dangerous to be pilots, and instructors needed to recognize them as early as possible. When we did, we would try to gently but firmly convince them that being a pilot was not for them. If you could not persuade them with words, there was another way to do this. We would let them fly themselves into a situation where the panic problem would manifest, and we would have to intervene to get them out of it. Few did not get the message after that happened.

As it came out during the confirmation hearings for Treasury Secretary Geithner, those who developed the TARP plan, and those who were in charge of implementing it, "panicked" in the crisis. "Panic" was Geithner's own word. Panic at the top is more than disconcerting—it is a sure sign that they either do not know what is happening or don't know what they are doing or both. This was one of the most disconcerting confirmation hearings I have personally ever followed. When Geithner was confirmed, it was not hard to predict the course that our economy would take, but it has been even worse than most expected. Without question, the inability to vet those whom we allow to steer our country is a major problem that needs to be fixed.

Some have described being a pilot as hours and hours of boredom interspersed by moments of sheer terror. We have terms for what pilots do when faced with this terror like "pinching a hole in the seat" to "If I had been sitting on a lump of coal I would have made a diamond!" You do tighten up, but you don't panic. To survive an emergency, you have to be proactive in a crisis, and you cannot shut down. Neither can you just start taking potshots at what might work. You have to stay cool enough to think and consider the probable results of any actions you take.

You can have the best form of government but still have bad government if you do not have good people in it. You can have the best, strongest, and safest plane ever built, and it can still be dangerous with a bad pilot at the controls. The wrong people can have the best motives but still not know what they're doing. Then you can have those who know what they're doing, but are prone to panic in a crisis. They can also have the best ideas, and know what to do, but not be able to do them because they panic. The great leaders, and the safest ones, are those who can stay cool and engaged in a crisis.

Too Cool

There was another kind of pilot who was just as dangerous as the ones who would panic—the overconfident. These could be even harder to deal with than the panic prone. As an instructor, I was assigned to help a Marine Corp fighter pilot get his civilian Airline Transport Rating. I knew he was going to be trouble when he introduced himself and started immediately telling me what a great pilot he was and that he was expecting to get chosen for the astronaut program soon. Sure enough I was not able to teach him anything because whenever I tried, he would take over the conversation and try to teach me.

After a few flights, this pilot started asking that I recommend him for the flight test because he did not need any more training. When I said he was not ready, he started demanding that I recommend him, accusing me of just wanting to make more money off of him. I would have paid *not* to have to work with him, but I knew he could not pass, so I went to the examiner for advice. He said to recommend him for the test anyway, so I did. He failed the first flight test of his life because he went the wrong way in a holding pattern. I was not surprised.

Then this pilot came back blaming me for not being a better instructor. I told him I was glad he failed because he might be good at dropping bombs on people, but he was too dangerous to actually carry people, which the civilian Airline Transport Rating could have enabled him to do. He left furious, and I was happy that I probably would not have to work with him anymore. A few days later he came back, not only teachable, but humble. I did not expect this. It was such a surprise to see him so changed that it was the beginning of my resolve to try to never give up on anyone because miracles of change do happen.

When I did eventually recommend this pilot to take the flight test again, he passed. I was also able to tell him I would trust him to fly me and my family anywhere. He was the only student I ever had who failed a flight test, but I think that failure taught me more than maybe all of my previous successes. I also think it probably made him an even better pilot and maybe a better officer.

To be a fighter pilot, or a test pilot, you must have an abundance of confidence, so I always tried to be careful when training fighter pilots to not hurt their confidence, but to pounce on arrogance as hard as I could. Confidence and arrogance are not the same thing. Confidence can help you in a crisis, but arrogance can blind you in it.

Those with a lot of pride are usually also the ones with the most initiative, and therefore, have the most potential. A basic rule of physics is that you cannot change the direction of something that is not moving. For this reason, I would much rather work with someone with pride than someone too self-deprecating. Could this be why Jesus chose disciples who would be arguing over who is the greatest even the night before He was crucified? He knew they were about to be humbled and would then be more trustworthy, but at least these disciples had enough initiative to want to be great and do great things.

It is right for America to want to be great and to do great things. At times, this has crossed over into pride, and we've paid a price for it. We need to learn from our mistakes, and how arrogance can hurt us, but keep our confidence and keep moving forward.

The Dangers of a Perfect Record

By owning an air charter service for a number of years, I was able to meet some of the most successful people in virtually every field. The oldest, wisest, and most successful almost all had a policy of not fully trusting anyone who had not failed yet. This wisdom is found in almost every religion, and those who do not heed it, usually pay a high price. One of the most dramatic examples of this was how The White Star Line chose Captain Smith to skipper the Titanic. It was because he had never had an accident at sea.

There can be more education in a single failure than from many successes. Virtually all of the greatest leaders in history had to overcome major, and often multiple, failures. This is true in American history as well. George Washington had a terrible failure in The French and Indian War. He was rejected for a commission in the British army. He then had repeated failures in the Revolutionary War, suffering many more defeats and only one real victory until he won the war at Yorktown. Abraham Lincoln failed at business and lost almost every election until he won the Presidency. Then he had many failures in his Presidency, but he did not panic nor did he quit, and he eventually saved the Union.

As a pilot, one of the really dumb things you can do is land without putting your landing gear down. This is not only embarrassing, but expensive, not to mention dangerous. However, there is a saying that there are pilots who have done this, and pilots who haven't *yet*. This implies that if you fly long enough, you will eventually do this. The safest pilots are usually those who have done this once. If they've done it twice, we obviously have a more serious problem. As they say, "There is no education in the second kick of a mule." Even so, the humility that comes from doing this once can last a lifetime and make for a much better, much safer pilot. And to answer what you are probably thinking, yes, I have done it too—but only once!

There is a story how in the early days of what are now the giant computer companies, there was an engineer who made a mistake that cost his company hundreds of thousands of dollars. When the president was asked if he was going to fire this man, his reply was, "No. I just spent several hundred thousand dollars educating him. Why should I do that and then give him to one of my competitors?"

The best leaders will almost always be those who have been tried through the fire of mistakes and failures. Proverbs, the biblical Book devoted to wisdom, says, **"For a righteous man falls seven times, and rises again" (see Proverbs 24:16).** The point is that those who have experienced repeated mistakes and failures, but who do not quit, will not only be some of the strongest possible leaders, but also the wisest.

Winston Churchill is another example of one who had many failures but did not quit and was ultimately used to save his nation. His blunders as head of the Admiralty in World War I were some of the most costly in Britain's military history; getting him fired and so maligned he would be ridiculed and scorned for the next 20 years by virtually the entire nation. No one ever expected him to recover from the public's ire, but later that same public would name him the greatest leader of the 20th century.

My point is that we cannot be too idealistic about our leaders either. Those who appear the most perfect may be the most dangerous. There are no perfect leaders, and often there are no perfect solutions to problems, so we just have to choose the best available.

It is shocking to learn that a high percentage of the most successful business people have been through a bankruptcy. Maybe that is why Jesus knew that Peter, who would fail so often, and even deny his Lord three times in one night, could be one of His greatest witnesses. I have as a personal policy that I will not give up on any person, but neither will I trust them with much until I see true humility, which almost never comes without some failure.

The point is that it may take someone who has been in the kind of ditch we're in now to get us out. In evaluating potential upcoming Presidential candidates, it is often said about some that they are not electable because of the mistakes they've made. Maybe that should be one of the criteria we're looking for to qualify them, not disqualify them. Certainly serious mistakes require scrutiny, but maybe in examining them we should look for how they acknowledged, understood, and were changed by their mistakes.

From the present Administration, the American public has been getting a crash course in learning that it is not what people say, but what they do that counts. When there is a serious and repeated disconnect between what a person says and does, there is a flaw that should disqualify him or her from leadership. This disconnect usually begins with not having the wisdom or humility to acknowledge mistakes, from which one can go on to the devastating delusion that he or she does not make mistakes. Those are headed for an iceberg that will take them down, so don't get on their ship.

We need those at the helm who have learned the wisdom that Proverbs says makes **"a righteous man"** the one who has fallen seven times but kept getting back up. Getting us out of the ditch we're in will likely require the leadership of someone who has been in the ditch before.

CHAPTER ELEVEN

KILLING US SOFTLY

Compassion is a great quality in a leader and a great quality in a nation. However, if it is not balanced with wisdom and experience, it can create more problems than it helps. This is the reason for the saying, "The road to hell is paved with good intentions."

Wrecking the Community

Some of the best-intended government programs to try to help people in need have not only been devastating to the needy, but to the nation. This is what led to the sub-prime crisis. The entire worldwide economic catastrophe that brought so many nations to the brink of a meltdown can be traced to the flawed policies in just one piece of Federal legislation—the Community Reinvestment Act (CRA).

This law was intended to help those who did not qualify to buy their own home because of their means or credit. This was a noble goal. It was not the goal that was flawed, but the method. This law forced banks and mortgage companies to make home loans—called "sub-prime" loans—to those who could not otherwise qualify for them. These people did not qualify for them for a reason, so this was inevitably going to ultimately lead to foreclosures. It did on a massive scale. This was the biggest factor that led to the economic meltdown we're still trying to recover from. Trying to help a few almost caused the bankruptcy of the entire world. It was that poorly thought out and implemented.

It took almost thirty years for the serious flaws in this legislation to fully manifest. Even though the signs were abundant that we were headed for a meltdown, Congress did nothing. Instead, the Senate and House committees in charge of Fannie Mae and Freddie Mac pressured lending institutions to make even more loans to sub-prime borrowers, exacerbating and speeding up the ultimate collapse of the real estate and mortgage industries.

The first problem this created was an expanding bubble that inflated real estate prices because so many were buying more house than they needed due to the mandated lower standards for getting a mortgage. This had a "trickle up" effect on the value of real estate, but there was no solid foundation to these values. You can only blow so much hot air into a balloon until it pops, and that's what happened.

The other critical problem created by this folly was by bankers and mortgage companies. Bankers have very accurate formulas for knowing which loans will default, and with so many borrowing far more than they should have been because of the CRA, they could foresee the coming losses. Knowing they had to do something to cover these losses or they would be in trouble, someone came up with the idea of bundling these mortgages into derivatives to sell as investment vehicles. This was just more hot air into the balloon.

Mortgage derivatives became increasingly popular investment vehicles, and rose in value, in some cases far beyond the appraised value of the property collateral of the mortgages. This created even more of an appetite for mortgage bundles, adding much more air to the housing bubble.

When the Chinese were approached with these derivatives that were being touted as a great investment opportunity, they looked at them, but refused to invest in them. They said that they did not invest in something they could not understand, and they could not understand why the derivatives were more valuable than the underlying collateral. Like the well-known fairytale, they were the first ones to tell the emperor that he did not have any clothes on. Quickly, everyone knew the emperor did not have any clothes on, and the markets tumbled. Virtually every major lending institution in the world had been caught up in this folly, and suddenly they were stuck with investments that were tanking fast.

Toxic Relief for Toxic Assets

This is a bit of an oversimplification, but it is essentially how the sub-prime crisis unfolded. As the sub-prime mortgages started defaulting, property values started collapsing. Quickly everyone who had taken the 100% financing or close to it were upside down in their mortgages, owing more, and in some cases much more than their property was worth. Banks and mortgage companies were taking back properties that they had lent more on than they were now worth, devastating their balance sheets. This forced them to shut down their lending windows because they could not take on any more risk while still holding so many loans and investments of dubious value. That forced the government to step in to stop the bleeding with the Toxic Asset Relief Program (TARP).

TARP was for the purpose of buying these toxic mortgages from the banks and lending companies to get them off of their books so they would be free to make loans again. This program was so poorly managed that the hundreds of billions of dollars appropriated for this seem to have just disappeared with little or none of the intended results. Our government, which is so prone to over-regulate virtually everything, basically gave this money out without any regulation, so those who got this money spent it on just about everything except what it was intended for. One of the largest American banks actually admitted to using some of the money they got from TARP to buy stock in the Chinese National Bank.

Since TARP did not work, it required hundreds of billions more for the bailouts. The bailouts were like free cocaine, and soon everyone was addicted and asking for more. This enabled many to fix their balance sheets without fixing the underlying problems, keeping us mired in deep financial problems, and everyone being hesitant to move forward.

America has suffered probably the greatest mismanagement of public resources in history for the last three quarters of a century, but in just the last two years, all of the previous folly was multiplied. It is no longer just mismanagement—it is financial insanity on an unprecedented level. As lending froze, markets tumbled, and housing continued to tank. Soon the auto makers and other big-ticket manufacturers were in trouble. Within a few months, just about everyone was in trouble because of the collapse of the housing bubble created by sub-prime lending intended to get people in more house than they could afford.

This is a simplified version of what happened, but it all started with our government compassionately trying to help everyone experience "the American dream" of owning their own home. Again, this was certainly a noble goal, and we should be thankful to have a government that cares enough about its people to try to help them. However, as government is prone to doing, this was so poorly managed that it has threatened to make everyone in the country poor. It has especially hurt the poor, who often left inferior houses, but ones they could afford, to buy those they could not afford, and now they don't have either.

Where does this mentality come from that there no longer needs to be qualifying, accountability, or responsibility? One basic way that some want to distribute wealth is to have the whole country subsidize loans for those who could not otherwise get them. We're doing that now with the tens of billions of dollars we must continue to give to the government mortgage outlets of Freddie Mac and Fannie Mae each year. Presently, there is no end in sight to how much more it will take to just clean up the mess that they've made, but our leaders keep pouring in more.

This illuminates the basic conflict between big government and small government reasoning. The good intentions of our government brought the world to the brink of economic collapse. Millions more have been hurt by this than were helped, and it is far from over. We are still dangling over the edge of a worldwide economic meltdown. If this happens, virtual worldwide anarchy will be followed by worldwide totalitarian tyranny, and all of it is unnecessary. Good intentions plus bad methodology have resulted in some of the world's biggest catastrophes.

The new Democratic Administration was quick to blame the banks and Wall Street for the crises, but the root of it was their own CRA. Certainly the banks and Wall Street do have some responsibility, especially with what they did with the derivatives, but the root of the problem was the Federal government's meddling, and then pressuring the lenders to make sub-prime loans.

Now, the legislation by which the government has asserted even more control over the whole financial industry is undercutting our basic freedoms, not just our strength and wealth as a nation. This was probably the biggest case in U.S. history of assigning the fox to watch the henhouse.

A Merger of Hope

The intention of liberals is often noble. It is the solutions they propose that can be so devastating. Leo Tolstoy addressed this in his classic novel *War and Peace*. In this novel, Count Pierre was a bleeding heart contending for the plight of the serfs, the Russian peasants. He sincerely cared about them but was such a poor manager that his own serfs were far worse off than Prince Andrei's. Prince Andrei was a good man, but was not driven as much by compassion as good business sense. Because of this, his estate was much better off than Pierre's; therefore, his serfs were also much better off. Who would you rather work for?

Certainly compassion is one of the highest human qualities, and greed is one of the lowest. The greatest economy would be one that balances compassion with good business sense. Maybe this is why the temple built by Solomon, who was said to be the wisest of all leaders, had two pillars—one named after a priest, Jakin, and one named after a businessman, Boaz. This was intended to be a reflection of the two pillars that God's throne was based on—righteousness and justice.

It was a part of the mandate of justice in the Old Testament for the wealthy to help the poor. It was not something they had to do—it was something they got to do. It was elevating, and it was an honor to help their fellow countrymen. We too should have that attitude, but because the government has taken this responsibility, not many people do anymore. It would only cost us a fraction of what we are now paying if the people would take this responsibility back.

Business leaders are generally portrayed as greedy, uncaring, with some even willing to scorch the earth for a profit. There are no doubt some in all of these categories, but there are also some who are the most generous people on the planet, even if it is because they have so much to be generous with. We now have two of the wealthiest men in the world, Bill Gates and Warren Buffett, giving away most of their fortunes to foundations they set up to help the less fortunate. This started a fad among the other super wealthy to do the same thing. The great hope is that these guys know how to manage the resources and can accomplish far more with them than the government ever could.

There are few things we can do that will make us feel better than helping others, and some even call it addictive. One of the best vehicles to beat back the follies of socialism is the generosity of the wealthy. The government does charity poorly and inefficiently, and we need to get the government out of it altogether. This cannot be done overnight, and we must be careful that people will not fall through the cracks in the transition, but if we really care about the less fortunate, we will find the way to take care of them without putting them at the mercy of the government.

We Can Do This

Good management is the answer to almost every economic problem we have now. If we applied it to our bloated government, putting it on a crash diet until it gets to the size that it should be, the deficits would be gone, and the economy would soar. If we can get this one thing, there is hope for a very bright future. We do not have to talk about radically changing anything else right now, including entitlements, if we are willing to make the substantial and necessary changes in just a few things—the size and efficiency of government.

Certainly entitlements need to be managed much better too. If managed correctly, it is likely the ultimate problems can be solved without cutting benefits or raising the age when people receive them. We could even end up giving people more than they are expecting. To date, when someone even begins to raise these solutions, they are shouted down and sometimes voted out of office for "attacking" Social Security or other entitlements. We, the American people, cannot keep falling to this purely political ploy.

It is time to insist on the debate and that it be done in the open. Let proposed solutions see the light of day. The longer we delay in addressing them, the more likely there will be cuts—and potentially even a meltdown of the whole system as we're seeing begin in Europe. The ultimate result of delaying longer will be that people will get nothing.

If we address basic size and efficiency in government and the management of entitlements, we will be on a much more stable, strong, and prosperous course. If we add basic tort reform to these, the result will be the biggest economic stimulus in history. This can lead to economic stability and health for generations to come.

Reaganomics, reducing taxes to stimulate the economy, works. Reagan borrowed the idea from John F. Kennedy. However, while reducing taxes, we must reduce the size of government too. While reducing the size, we must change the culture of government to one of efficiency and effectiveness with every job it is given by the American people.

Chapter Twelve

BUREAUCRATS AND LAWYERS

Most bureaucrats are not the villains. They are not responsible for letting the government get so huge and inefficient that it is now consuming the nation's resources. In many cases, they are the worst victims of the system. Some should be considered heroes for being able to accomplish anything in the present mire of overregulation and red tape.

In the culture of government today, one must have extraordinary focus and resolve to accomplish anything. Take the shackles off of our bureaucrats and many would be able to do many times what they are now. Those who are of such resolve can be the leaders in straightening out the mess and will appreciate even more the necessary changes in government. The public service unions have the most of all to lose if we do not tackle this crisis of inefficiency and incompetence in government. They can work for improvement and be heroes of the American people, or they will become the biggest villains of the American people for being obstructionists for what simply has to be done.

The Question

If we implemented the kind of efficiency we're talking about and reduced the size of the Federal government to 20% of its present size, it will be understandable that many might ask, "Won't that swell the ranks of the unemployed?" The answer to that is "no" because to do this right it would have to be done over time, probably 10 years. A goal of 10% reduction a year would probably be optimum.

When we take the shackles of overregulation and unnecessary taxes off of the economy and channel the trillions of dollars back into it that is now consumed in the black hole of government, one of our biggest problems will be not having enough people for the jobs. Many of those now serving government will need to shift to the private sector, but the demand for them will be huge, and everyone will ultimately benefit much more from efficiency in government.

What About Lawyers?

The majority of our representatives in government are lawyers. Certainly lawyers have a crucial place in modern civilization, but there is nowhere else on earth where they have come to so dominate the culture as they do in the U.S. at this time. The consequences of the legalistic mentality, and especially the out-of-control lawsuits, are as much a threat to our future as the out-of-control deficits. We are at the breaking point with the legal entanglements America is now tied down by, and this too must be changed.

We need leadership. However, the qualities that make one a good leader and those that make one a good lawyer are contrary to each other. Some lawyers have become effective leaders, but they usually leave the legal profession to do so because they weren't that great at being a lawyer. As stated earlier, a legal mentality tries to resolve problems with laws, but a leader will simply lead through the problem. Some situations may require a new law, but many don't. When we make unnecessary laws, we usually resolve a situation for a few people while making life much harder for millions of others. We can all think of laws like this.

During the Carter Administration, Alexander Solzhenitsyn, the great Russian author, dissident, and sage gave a speech at Harvard University that shook the entire nation. It was titled, "A World Split Apart" and was probably the most powerful oration given in America since Martin Luther King, Jr. gave his "I Have a Dream" speech. Solzhenitsyn prophetically addressed the great spiritual and moral breakdown in the world and especially focused on what he saw potentially dooming America. His prophecy has come to pass, and we stand now at the edge of the collapse he foresaw.

Solzhenitsyn spent a good deal of his life in the Soviet Gulag or prison culture in Siberia. His writings had been smuggled out and published, making him a world figure and voice so powerful that the Soviet Union could not kill him or keep him in prison without serious repercussions from world opinion. They decided to exile him to America. Solzhenitsyn thought that he was coming to the Promised Land, but was quickly shocked by what he found. He was able to see the rottenness attacking our foundations, which he addressed in this speech with the clarity and power of an Old Testament prophet. The nation was so shaken that his speech was carried on the front page of almost every major newspaper, and even then President Carter had to make a statement about it.

Solzhenitsyn saw legalism displacing our basic potential to do good, and that it would eventually choke us to death if we did not reverse it. To date we have not turned from it, and its grip is tightening around our throat. (This speech is contained as an addendum at the end of this book.)

As I shared before, when I owned an air charter service I was able to meet some of the most successful people in just about every field. I flew Presidential candidates, entertainers, leading sports figures, military leaders, but mostly business leaders. I studied them all because I wanted to understand what enabled people to be successful. One common denominator with all of the top leaders I met was that they did not let their lawyers run their businesses. They had lawyers, and they listened to their counsel, but the most successful would tell me that once your lawyer started controlling you, it was not likely that you could stay on the cutting edge of progress, and they could bring you to ruin. All but a few lawyers simply had a mentality that was incongruent with the basic faith, vision, and initiative required for success in almost any endeavor—except politics in America.

We should appreciate lawyers in their place, and value their counsel, but I too learned as a young businessman that if I was going to succeed, I could not let them run my business. I have watched businesses where the lawyers were able to gain dominant influence, and I've never seen good results from this. They're needed, but they should not be leading. They should not be leading our government. Our government is now basically a lawyers' club. Whenever this is allowed, we will get what we see unfolding in the country. California is a good example. The State of California is bankrupt, but 725 new laws were imposed on Californians on New Year's Day 2011.

Why can't the Administration, or Congress, see issues that are so clear to a majority of Americans? They see through a legalistic lens. The legalism in America is unnatural and considered way out of bounds even in the bureaucratic European Union. No other country on earth is being so strangled legalistically as America is now.

Politicians vs. Leaders

Politicians are a species that is unnatural and should be made extinct. There is certainly a place for skilled negotiations, and knowing how to bring groups together with different and sometimes conflicting interests, but being a politician should not define anyone's basic nature or profession. Regardless of what they may say, professional politicians see everything through one lens, which is how they can get elected or re-elected. That is a lens that will make anyone demented. We need leaders leading who see through one lens—what is best for the nation and its people.

In Scripture, it says where **"selfish ambition exists, there is disorder and every evil thing" (see James 3:16).** Selfish ambition destroys the kind of vision required for leadership in a republic. Once in office, or in a bureau, they must keep first the good of the people, not just what protects their interests or position. If we had this kind of true public servant in service, we would have a far different and a far better government than we do now.

Again, our Republic was never intended to become the domain of professional politicians. This rogue species was greatly feared by the Founders, and we are now experiencing the troubles they foresaw if such a group gained a foothold in our government, much less dominate it as they now do. Our representatives were to be citizens who served as a duty, part-time, and live in the real world with the rest of us so they too would have to live with the laws they passed. Having to live with their own laws, and the people they impose them on, would certainly change many of their actions.

Some contend that the business of government is just too complicated and requires full-time representatives now. I would counter if they only passed 10% to 20% of the laws that are really necessary, written in plain English, they would only need to be there 10% to 20% of the time that they're in session now.

The culture in Washington has become such that America is far better off, and far safer, when Congress is not in session. The next time Congress has a session, it should be to remove archaic and bad laws from the books, not pass new ones. We should measure the success of a Congress by the laws they undid instead of the legislation passed. Maybe we should consider passing a law that two laws have to be taken off of the books for every one that is passed until reason has been restored.

Citizen representatives, who themselves have to live by the laws they pass and who do not get all of the perks they've voted for themselves at our expense, are the only way a republic can last long without falling to the corruption, waste, and inefficiency we now have in our government. The system is out of control, is far from what it was intended to be, and cannot last as it is much longer unless it returns to its intended design. It has fallen to us to do this—to begin a second American Revolution that returns us to the wisdom and sanity of the results of the first one.

It is not a matter of whether we *can* do this but whether we *will* do it. We need the leadership, management, and the will to get it done.

The Root of Evil

America has now crossed the line into the depth of depravity that we are told in Isaiah and other Scriptures will lead to the doom of a nation—when evil is called good, and good is called evil, where the honorable man is dishonored, and the dishonorable are honored (see Isaiah 5:20). Not long ago America was possibly the most moral country on earth, but in America right now morality is scorned, and even persecuted, while immorality is flaunted and honored. As the Scripture points out, this is the last state of a nation before destruction. Without a true revival in America, fixing the economy, and even fixing our government, will not be enough.

As discussed earlier, recent figures indicate that about 80% of Americans consider themselves to be Christians, and many of the rest are devoted to religions with high moral standards. Yet America has fallen into its worst state of debauchery ever, with the tragic result being a destruction of the core strength of any great nation—the family. The first thing that God said was **"not good"** was for man to be alone (see Genesis 2:18), and He gave mankind family as a remedy to this. Loneliness can bring out the worst in people, and without strong families we simply will not survive. We have now fallen to such debauchery that to many, pro-family talk is considered "hate speech" against homosexuals.

I was a delegate to The World Public Forum on Civilizations and Religions (WPF). It is one of the most remarkable gatherings possibly in history. Present and former government leaders, top academics, and top leaders of all of the major religions meet at the WPF each year for several days of dialog. Top Islamic leaders attend from probably every major Muslim country, as well as rabbis, and leaders of Hinduism, Buddhism, and other major religions. Christianity was represented mostly by Catholic and Orthodox delegates, and

I was one of only three or four evangelicals. Over the days I was able to spend considerable time with some of these leaders, but I was especially interested in those from Islam because of the issue it now is for the whole world. Understanding comes from the term "to stand under" someone else's position, and I especially wanted to know why so many hated America so much.

I was surprised that every one of these leaders that I talked to was unaware of evangelical Christianity or had a very skewed view of what it actually is. They were surprised in my speech when I apologized for the moral perversion that was being exported from America through our movies and television. They thought that the movies coming out of Hollywood were a representation of American Christianity. This was one of the main reasons why they considered us "the great Satan," because we claimed to worship God but exported the worst kind of moral depravity to the nations. They felt in America, Europe, and wherever Western civilization dominated that immorality was so deep that such depravity could only be remedied by destroying us. Those from Islam, and even some of the other religious leaders, thought that America was a homosexual nation controlled by homosexuals. When I tried to explain that this was just a tiny portion of the population, they simply could not fathom such a small group having such dominance over our culture.

The basic lines between good and evil have never been more blurred in America. Moral relativism has reduced us, Europe, and much of Western civilization to a confused and self-destructing shell of what made us great. We have determined that if something is legal, then it must be right or at least alright to practice. Truth and integrity have been sacrificed on the altar of our increasing hedonism. Many of our own citizens have started to say that truth, integrity, and basic morality have been so destroyed in America that we may be beyond saving.

Truth, integrity, and morality have not been totally destroyed in America, but they have probably never been under such attack. Even so, at times America has been in worse shape, even tolerating slavery. We are in desperate shape and still sliding downhill fast, but there is hope. Great Awakenings have come to America before to save her out of the most desperate of times, and we can be saved out of our present darkness too.

We have two entirely different roads before us now. If we continue to turn in the direction we have been going for the last half century, our time as a great nation, and maybe even as a nation, will be over soon. If there is an awakening among those who have been given the knowledge of righteousness and justice, and a resolve among those awakened to boldly stand for the truth they have been entrusted with, America's best times will be ahead of us.

When we discuss morality, most people automatically think of sexual morality. Of course that is important, as is basic integrity with such things as keeping our vows, speaking the truth, honoring our word, and so forth. However, as we have also discussed, it has been estimated that as much as half of the teachings on righteousness in the Bible are about stewardship—good management of the resources we have been entrusted with. Morality and good stewardship are not mutually exclusive, but are in fact joined at the hip.

A devotion to truth, integrity, and morality will be revealed in our economy. This was so important to Jesus that in the Parable of the Talents He taught that the one who would be called the **"wicked, lazy slave"** was the servant who did not manage well what was entrusted to him. The servant who was told, **"Well done, good and faithful servant,"** was the one who had managed well what had been entrusted to him (see Matthew 25:21-26).

All of the standards of righteousness and sin in Scripture are based on the impact of behavior on people. Waste is sin because it hurts people. Great waste is an even greater sin because more people are hurt by it. Presently, the U.S. Government is the most wasteful, inefficient entity on the planet. How many people are being hurt by this, or how many are not being helped who could be?

CHAPTER THIRTEEN
THE HOLE IN THE SHIP

As discussed, it does not matter what your job is on a ship; if the ship gets a hole in it then everyone becomes a part of the damage-control team. The American ship of state now has a number of holes in it that are taking on water, but the biggest of all is the economy. If this hole is not fixed soon, then all of our social and other agendas are not going to be relevant.

The economy itself has a number of crises. One of the most critical holes in the economy is the plummeting value of the dollar. Some weakening of the dollar can help trade, but the collapse of the dollar could sink the whole ship of state, and that is now a real possibility. Because the dollar has nothing backing it but faith in the American government and economy, when faith in these are lost, people, even Americans, will stop taking the dollar. This would bring unprecedented chaos to America.

If the U.S. dollar survives much longer, it will be a surprise to some of the greatest financial minds in the world. Some think that the only reason the dollar has not already collapsed is there just is nowhere else for the world to go at this time. That may be true, but it's changing. Other economies and currencies are starting to rival America. The present Administration has been reduced to almost begging these governments to keep buying our debt and keep taking the dollar. The security of our nation is that precarious at this writing.

Some think that the Obama Administration is purposely trying to kill the dollar so that we can go to a one-world currency and bring the U.S. gradually under subjugation to the international community. Such treason actually being committed by our President is too unthinkable to even consider without clear and irrefutable evidence, but the foolish economic policies being pursued by the Administration seem to be making such a fate for the dollar inevitable. The newly-elected Republican-controlled House that seems willing to fight any more spending, and possibly lock down the debt ceiling, may have saved the dollar, at least for a time.

The "orderly" destruction of the U.S. dollar has been a publicly stated goal of the multi-billionaire financier that many think has been controlling the Democratic Party—George Soros. Could one man actually collapse the currency of the strongest nation on earth? Yes. With the kind of hedging and leveraging that can be done now, this can be accomplished with a tiny percentage of what we might think would otherwise be necessary. However, Soros does not have to do this alone because there are many with the goal of bringing America down, and they know that collapsing the dollar can do it.

Internationalists like Soros believe the U.S. is the greatest obstacle to the future world order they envision. Actually some in our country, and even in our government, have openly stated they believe the best thing for the world is neutralizing the U.S. Soros has been blamed for collapsing several European currencies, including devastating the British pound, and many think his ultimate goal is to collapse the American dollar in order to remove America as the obstacle to world unity. Whether he is the one pulling the strings or not, the dollar is under an unrelenting assault.

Why would the extremely wealthy like Soros want a socialist or Marxist takeover since they obviously would be the biggest losers? First, idealism does not always make sense. Second, Marxism just wipes out the middle class and the elite rule the rest. Obviously, those like Soros see themselves as being a part of this elite. However, in Marxist takeovers people like Soros would be eliminated very fast regardless of how much they helped the revolution. Powerful, assertive people cannot be tolerated under totalitarianism.

The Hot, Cold War

In Chapter Two we discussed the four great powers of the earth, and that we are now in the Economic epoch where the wars are Economic wars, and the most powerful leaders are Economic leaders. The weapons in these wars are Economic more than Military, and America, the most powerful nation in the world economically, has been in retreat in this war for a long time. We must have new leadership that can understand and fight this very real war. The lack of leadership has put our very survival in jeopardy, but with the right leadership America still has the power to turn this around and be victorious in it.

Recently, two of the biggest and most important governments in the world, Russia and China, agreed to use their own currencies for trade rather than the dollar. For a long time we have been concerned that China would do this, but for Russia and China to do this together was devastating news for our dollar. Some have even called it fatal for the dollar. It does not have to be fatal, but no doubt it is a devastating blow.

When our President gets chastised by the heads of Britain, France, Germany, Russia, and China for taking the U.S. toward socialism, it should be a wake-up call to all Americans.

When China refuses to keep buying our bonds and starts to divest those they are holding—chiding our President for the foolish economic course he's taking—this should be a wake-up call to all Americans.

Some of the greatest economic thinkers in the world have been saying that the course we are now on is the worst of all scenarios, and we have been following it like a sheep to slaughter. No administration,

Republican or Democratic, has made a serious effort to correct the root of our economic problems—government that has grown out of control, causing untenable deficits, and costing us greatly in what every economy needs to be stable and successful, which is faith in it. Our present Administration has sought to fix the economy by feeding the very cancer that is killing it—growing the government more than any President in history as well as the deficits more than all previous Presidents. That's right. Our deficits have grown more in the last two years than in the last two hundred and fifty years combined.

At this writing, no part of the private sector has had job growth in more than two years, while the government has grown dramatically. The "brain cancer" that our government has is now causing more than annoying headaches—it is threatening to kill us very quickly. We do not have time to ignore this any longer.

Changing from a Democratic "big government" to a Republican "small government" administration is not enough to remedy the condition we are now in. To date, Republicans have done very little to cut government or government spending. For a long time there has been a disconnect between what just about anyone in government says and what they actually do. We cannot trust their words any longer but must examine closely what they actually do.

Our government is not just obese and putting too much strain on our heart—it is more like one of those who have grown to 800 pounds! Our government is now about 80% fat. We are in a desperate emergency. We need radical surgery, followed by a radical diet, and exercise that gets us back to being the kind of example of what good government should be like that exists to serve the people.

As the mid-term elections of 2010 proved, no conservative politician in history has so united the conservatives and moderates in this nation as Obama has. The Republicans were the immediate benefactors of the transformation now going on in the mentality of the nation, but this could be short-lived. Americans are fed up with both parties, and for good reason. The necessity and the movement in America for radical change are bouncing off of most politicians who are only thinking from a political perspective.

There now are some encouraging signs that the kind of changes required to restore our economic health may be made because public support for them has gone on to become public demand. The awakening has begun, and there are good indications that there will not be a letup, but rather the opposite—momentum is building for more.

The Great Fallacy

Because government does not produce anything marketable, everyone who works for the government has to be supported by someone in the private sector who is producing something marketable. Marketable products are our tax base. Therefore, producing government jobs is not nearly as important as producing private sector jobs that produce marketable goods or services. Presently, over 40% of Americans either work for government on some level, or derive their income from government. This means that someone who is a producer now has to produce enough to provide for themselves and their family, and just about fully take care of a government employee and their family too. No economy has been able to sustain even close to this kind of ratio for long, and ours won't last that much longer in this state either.

It gets worse! If the Obamacare legislation is not repealed, then the ranks of government workers will soon exceed 50% of the population. Before Obamacare was passed, healthcare was a major market export, with many from around the world coming here to get the best healthcare in the world. If Obamacare is fully implemented, there is no way that we will not have rationing, turning another producer for America into just another consumer, and a very big one.

Our economy is struggling to survive the present load, and it simply cannot survive Obamacare. The healthcare legislation will not be "the straw that breaks the camel's back;" it's like dropping a Sherman tank on the back of the already overloaded camel.

Our economy is under assault from within and without. It is like trying to fight off a major attack with saboteurs also hitting us from within our own ranks. It may seem impossible to win a battle like this, but it has been done before. Some of the decisive military battles in history were won by extraordinary leaders who faced the crises of having saboteurs in their own ranks, while being greatly outnumbered by the enemy they faced at the same time. We're being hit hard and often from within and without, but we can still win and come out of this conflict stronger than ever. Never, never, never give up.

Chapter Fourteen
FOUNDATION FOR PROSPERITY

Justice is the basis for stability in any nation or economy. The stronger and more consistent the system of justice, the stronger and more prosperous the economy, and indeed the nation, is likely to be. One of the primary reasons for the strength and enduring success of America has been its overall integrity and consistency. This was the result of our basic commitment to contract law. We may have too many laws, but at least they were what you could count on to be upheld in any court. Because of this, America was considered one of the safest places in the world to do business. In 2009 this sense of safety was shattered.

Almost immediately after the inauguration in 2009, our government started changing the rules and canceled contracts without due process. This quickly changed America from a very dependable place to do business to one considered undependable. Economic initiative disappears in an atmosphere of instability. Changing the rules had the immediate chilling effect worldwide that America was no longer a stable, trustworthy business environment. No wise investor will put their money where they can't count on consistency in the rules or in the behavior of the government.

Stability

The friendliest environment for commerce is consistency in wise regulations and stability in government. These allow those who are putting their resources at risk to be able to reasonably forecast future conditions and therefore have more faith in their plans. You can have many other opportunities, but if you don't have these two basic factors, it will be hard to attract quality business ventures.

The basic role of government in an economy is to be the referee that keeps business on a level, fair playing field. Some rules are needed or no one could play the game. For the best conditions, the rules should be easy to understand and applied evenly, fairly, and consistently. A good referee should be as unobtrusive as possible to let the players play the game but present enough to enforce the rules and be ready to step in when there are violations.

Think about what would happen if a referee started changing the rules in the middle of the game. All of your strategy for winning the game may suddenly be wrong, causing you to lose. Doing this would cause, at best, increasing hesitancy on the part of everyone playing the game. This is what happened to business in America in 2009—the rules started being changed without warning.

Then think how much worse it would be if the referees started changing the rules and making them retroactive! You thought you had won just to find out you had lost because of new rules you were not even told about. Obviously, this would make it very hard to get anyone to play such a game. This is what happened to business in America in 2009. Rules were changed arbitrarily by the Administration, using executive orders, and some were actually made retroactive. This was a most shocking departure from the basic integrity and consistency of our system, and then the Administration seemed dumbfounded at why their touted recovery never got going! Why would anyone want to start hiring and getting back into the game in such an environment? We should be thankful for all those businesses that stayed in the game, but this kind of behavior threatens our continued existence as a Republic.

To cover for its decisions, the Administration started putting much of the blame on the banks for the stagnation of the economy.

However, the Administration itself has been forcing conditions on the banks that hindered their ability to be aggressive and may actually destroy many of them. Some banking reform is needed, but the draconian reform the government has imposed is almost sure to kill them, not heal them.

As we touched on before, the recent Financial Reform Act has almost certainly doomed the small community banks if it is not radically changed or repealed. Small community banks are the lifeblood of small business, and what is being done to them now will doom our future. Every big business started as a small one, and our future economic health depends on a healthy atmosphere for the creation of small business to keep the pipeline of our economic lifeblood flowing. An economy without small business is like a society without children—it is ultimately doomed to oblivion.

Now back to our game where the rules are being changed at the whim of the officials, with some even being made retroactive. Not many would want to play such a game, but some did continue. Now think of how the game would degenerate even further if a referee not only started changing the rules at his whim, but started jumping in to play the game. It would be like watching a football game and having the referee intercept the ball and run for a score and give it to the other team. That would surely shut the game down or make it so confusing no one would want to play it. That is what happened when our government took over General Motors and Chrysler, putting their own people on the boards of our banks, and so forth. Then they continue to wonder why the economy is still stuck in the ditch!

Since 2009 business in America has been traumatized. Many in business are only continuing in the game because they are betting that the Administration is going to change soon and that a reasonably fair game will be recovered. It must happen or we are headed for much worse than just a decline.

Still in the Ditch

The 2010 election results gave many hope that stability would be returning. The economy responded about as well as anyone could have hoped. Even so, every wise and experienced business person in America knows that we are still in the ditch. The radical jerk to the left in 2009 will at the very least leave many with the jitters for a long time. America had never been as unpredictable as we became in 2009. It is a tribute to the resilience of our economy that there were not many more catastrophic results. The push back by the American people has caused the Administration to back off some in the direction they were going, but their actions have already caused problems that could last for a long time.

The Administration had set such a hostile tone to business that more of our core industries started locating abroad, and there has been a large flight of capital from the U.S. since 2009. This may have subsided when the American people began to push back, making it likely the perpetrators of these anti-business policies would soon be voted out. However, the country is not that excited about a Republican takeover either. The changes that are needed are profound changes in our government. The economy will be fine if the government will stay out of the game, except to be the good referee it is supposed to be.

The Lynchpin of Progress

Congress is where the people of the United States have the most direct influence over their government. Much of the instability in our country now is the result of the erosion of the power of Congress by the other two branches of government. In our Constitution, Congress alone has the power to make laws. The President has been usurping congressional authority by using executive orders, and the judicial branch has been usurping it by legislating from the bench. The consequences have become increasingly dangerous, and the authority of Congress must be restored if there is to be lasting and deep stability restored.

With the present low approval rating of Congress, many may think we don't want them having any more power, but the system will not work without a strong Congress. A primary reason for its low approval rating is because it has been so weak and yielding to do the Administration's work, and often its dirty work, instead of being the strong voice of the people and a check and balance on the Executive and Judicial branches that it was mandated to be.

Congress is not elected to serve the President, but the people. Of course, the President is elected to do this also, but our Founders knew very well that "power corrupts," and they mandated that there would be a very powerful check on Executive power—the Congress.

Because no leadership of the stature required to do this has arisen in Congress, it will likely take a strong President to correct this. To date no President seems willing to give up any authority, much less purposely restore the congressional authority that most Presidents are in a constant battle with. Even so, this alone can prevent the continuing overreach of the Executive and Judicial branches, and provide for the long-term health and stability of the nation. We have been moving strongly toward an imperial presidency in which Congress will eventually be just a meaningless window dressing and rubber stamp for the Administration. This trend is a very basic threat to our freedom and our stability.

Recovery

Any enterprise takes faith. The actions of our government lately could hardly have been more devastating to the kind of faith that it takes for enterprise and initiative. When you start changing the rules by executive order, and then making some of them retroactive, it is the beginning of totalitarianism. When our government decided they were not going to just be referees, but play the game themselves, taking over some of our largest companies, and then one of our largest industries with healthcare, we slid much further toward totalitarianism. The American people have started waking up and pushing back. In 2010, the American people took a major step toward taking back. The hope is that the push back continues until the necessary radical changes needed in government are completed.

Even if government could manage the industries it seized, the takeover of these is scary. With the government's disastrous lack of management skills, this has terrifying long-term implications. We are following a similar pattern that was followed in the 1930s that kept the nation mired in The Great Depression until the war picked us back up. After the crash of 1929, there was a comeback that looked like a recovery. It was cut off by similar government overreach as we've seen in the last two years, and by 1932 the downward spiral was tightening into a death spiral that took a great war to stop.

If you will bear with another pilot's metaphor, comparing the American economy to a plane, it has been hovering very close to a stall, which if not corrected can result in a spin, which if not corrected can result in a "death spiral" few ever recover from. Let me explain briefly these terms. A stall occurs when you get so slow there is not enough air passing over your wings to maintain the lift required to hold your altitude, so you start falling out of the sky. If you are in a stall and bank hard to the left or right, you will enter a spin. If the spin tightens too much, it can become a "death spiral" that is very hard to recover from. If you keep lifting the nose of the plane while in a stall instead of pushing it forward, you can enter a flat spin where even with your falling there is still not enough air moving over your wings to regain control.

In 2008, our economy was like a plane that went into a stall. We lost the forward speed required to keep the lift we needed. The answer to the problem was to push the nose forward and add power to get the speed up enough to create the lift needed to keep us airborne. The Administration did the opposite, holding back on the nose, creating a flat spin and then kicking the rudder hard left and making the spin even worse. This was the worst thing that could have been done, and it's why we went zooming past the 8% unemployment everyone feared to nearly 10%. We have not been able to climb back to where we were. We entered an economic flat spin.

The 2010 elections added some right rudder that seems to have at least slowed the spinning. It may seem like we're in something of a recovery now, but from the instruments I'm looking at, we are at the very least still hanging on the edge of a stall. If the Administration kicks us hard to the left again, we are now at such a low altitude we could be in trouble. The elections of 2010 may have checked the turning to the left, but we are still at a precariously slow speed and could enter the spin again easily.

Every pilot practices stall recovery over and over. You learn to recognize an imminent stall so you can recover even before it happens. To recover, you need to level your wings, add power, and if necessary push the nose over to gain more speed, therefore creating more wind over the wings to increase lift again. Then, you regain your altitude but only fast enough to maintain a speed that keeps you safely away from another stall.

If you have gone from a stall to a spin, you do all of the above while also kicking in the opposite rudder of the direction of the spin. To get out of our spin to the left we will need to kick in some right rudder until the turning has been stopped. Then, as we are safely out of the spin and stall, we need to gradually get back on course, only gently turning until we are in stable, level flight.

I am a conservative, but I realize an eagle needs both a left and right wing to fly. Therefore, I try to respect and learn from other people's opinions even if I am on the other side of issues. I must be somewhere near the middle, or just right of center, because I can see people about equally as far out to both the left and the right, but a little farther out to the left. I am as concerned about going too far to the right as I am too far to the left. I may be a fighter pilot at heart, and I love aerobatics, but when I'm carrying passengers, my goal is the smoothest, most gentle flight possible, with no steep banks. This is how the pilot, or President, has to think for the sake of the people.

The present rising up of the American people with the demand to straighten up is very encouraging. What we do not want to do is overcorrect and spin off to the right. We are a center/right nation, and there is a danger of overcorrecting to the extreme right. The center is often associated as the place of compromise, but in many ways the right course is between the extremes. As stated, biblically there is a "path of life" that is found between the extremes of legalism on one side and lawlessness on the other. The extremes on the left and right are the ditches on either side of the right path for America.

What Not to Do

Right now we are still moving too slow and are dangling far too close to another stall/spin scenario. The biggest struggle that will likely decide whether we recover fully, or again fall into a downward spiral, will be whether the government takeover of healthcare can be reversed. If you want examples of how the government can run business, just look at Amtrak or the Postal Service. Then you might want to think of the last time you had to deal with any government bureaucracy. Now think about that experience while trying to deal with a serious health issue. Is that something we want our parents, or our children, to face?

If that does not scare you, remember how the "death panels" so outraged America that they had to be dropped from the healthcare reform legislation? Over the 2010 Christmas holidays, the Administration slipped them back in by Executive Order while everyone was out of town and no one would notice. Why is this so important to this Administration? Why is the government so intent on getting its citizens to go to a government bureaucracy for end-of-life counseling? This should be most sobering to every American, especially the elderly.

Now back to the two biggest government-run enterprises—Amtrak and the Postal Service. They each lose billions every year, which we pay for. They don't have to be accountable and make a profit or provide good service because our tax dollars are propping them up. Why is it that all of the private sector companies that are in the package delivery business have done so well, but the government can't? Government has proven 100% of the time that it cannot manage anything well that it tries to manage. Why do we even consider letting it take over anything else? This has to be one of the most persistent cases of Einstein's definition of insanity. The only other conclusion may be that some have a different agenda for the world that cannot abide a strong America, and are therefore following Saul Alinsky's *Rules for Radicals* strategy for destroying America. 2009 and 2010 have unfolded just like Alinsky's book. Is it a coincidence? Perhaps. Whether it is intentional or not, the basic fabric of American strength is being unraveled just like the plan in that book.

Even with all of our problems America was the best place in the world to invest until 2008. Now much of the smart money even in America is leaving to invest in Asia where it is considered safer. This is one of the worst economic tragedies of our times, and it did not happen overnight. It did hit overdrive in 2009. If the nationalization of healthcare is accomplished, it is unlikely that our economy, or our political system, can survive long.

Some argue that European nations have done pretty well with this model, but have they? Europe is starting to unravel just like America, along with every other nation that goes down that road. The only reason why the European Union has not imploded to date is because it has been carried on the back of the German economy. Germany is still easily manipulated because of their guilt after World War II, but the emerging generation in Germany is not going to put up with this much longer.

With such recent clear examples of government overreach, and the citizens rising up and getting more intent to put restraints on the government so that it cannot do this again, there is hope. We can rebuild the world's business trust in America again. If we can navigate out of the present stall, get our speed up again, and our altitude, we have a great plane that can take us much farther still.

Chapter Fifteen
THE NEW MARXISTS

It is remarkable that there are still Marxists in the world when the economic policies it espouses have been proven such a fallacy. In every case where Marxism has been embraced, usually through movements in disgruntled lower classes, these lower classes became victims just like everyone else and are usually the ones most oppressed by it. It seems to always be true that "those who do not know history are doomed to repeat it." However, there is more to the phenomenon of why there are still Marxists in the world. Marxism can only take root where there is real injustice and especially where the wealthy oppress the lower classes.

"Social justice" is a powerful term, but whenever it has been used for insurrection it has never resulted in justice, but only another form of injustice that is even worse. The social justice philosophy is basically about the redistribution of wealth, but forced redistribution has proven to only destroy wealth and then leave everyone poor. Even so, justice is an issue that must be paramount, or we will never have true stability or security.

Marxism has been most effective in gaining traction where it can sow an entitlement mentality in the lower classes. The entitlement mentality is a basic disconnect between earning, effort, initiative, and reward. This is a seedbed for envy, which may be the ugliest of all pollutions of the human soul. We are told in Scripture that even Jesus was crucified because of envy (see Matthew 27:18). When the entitlement mentality is promoted by politicians promising more in order to get elected, the result of this will always be bigger social problems, and ultimately lawlessness and riots like we're starting to see across Europe. (We will look at how entitlements and lawlessness are connected in a later chapter.)

Some excesses and injustices in America have provided the soil for Marxist philosophy to take some root here. It was a shock to the nation to see huge bonuses given to company executives right after these companies received bailouts from the government and right after laying off thousands of people. This could not help but to feed outrage in the public. We must not forget that real justice is the only true and lasting counter to the delusions that are called by such terms as "social justice."

True economic justice will maintain an open path to advancement from the bottom of the economic food chain all the way to the top. It will promote respect for everyone at every position along the process and a healthy rejection of excesses and abuses.

The government was at least partly to blame for this travesty of how so much of our hard-earned tax dollars went to these extreme bonuses to the bailed out companies. Our insanely over-regulating government gave out the stimulus money with seemingly no conditions about how it was to be used. Such mismanagement is what we have to expect from our government at this time. This kind of a lack of restraint with those companies also hurt everyone but especially the business community.

Education and Injustice

The most disgruntled people in the world who trend toward a socialist agenda are usually the least educated and the most educated. Why are they at each extreme like this? The less educated are often the poor and struggling, and this can be a seedbed for discontent. The highly educated who are socialists usually are

124

because the basic strategy of Marxism in America was to infiltrate education and sow it in every textbook if possible, and they have done this very effectively.

We now have history books in American public schools that do not have one honorable thing to say about American history. Instead they highlight the failures and injustices such as slavery, the treatment of the Native Americans, and so forth. Some then go on to glorify many of the worst enemies of democracy and freedom.

A major question we should have is: Should we, the American people, continue to pay for our children to be educated by anti-American propagandists who actually seek our downfall? Our very freedoms may allow for such an education, but it is outrageous that the American people are now made to pay for it, and it is virtually the only public education available. Possibly the most important position concerned Americans should be seeking election to are our school boards. Then we need to mobilize parents and other concerned citizens to read every textbook.

I would never imply that textbooks on things like history should leave out the failures, but neither should it leave out the good. Our students can now go all the way through public school without hearing one good thing about their own country. They are being taught to be America haters instead of good citizens. There may have never been another nation in history with as much good to talk about, or another nation that is doing as much good around the world right now as America is, and it is outright deception not to include it in our history courses or in the media.

Because of the effectiveness of this strategy to infiltrate education in America, especially through our textbooks, many have taken on Marxist beliefs and do not even know it. "Social justice" as it is usually taught is a Marxist philosophy. Even so, the best way to counter this is with the truth and justice. True justice will never be afraid of the truth. The truth of history makes the results of Marxism very clear, and they also make clear the traps we need to avoid in the future that are on both the left and the right.

In an open society like we still have, truth will eventually prevail. The Marxist strategy to sow their philosophy throughout our education system is beginning to backfire now. Many who have been educated with the continuous anti-American and socialist propaganda have not only started to hear the other side of the story—they are energetically seeking it out. The growing desire to know the truth about American history is resulting in books on the subject now climbing the bestseller lists. Those who wake up to "the other side of the story" will not be so easily fooled again.

Ancient Wisdom

As we discussed earlier, one of the basic precepts of justice in the Old Testament was that the wealthy had an obligation to consider and help the poor and oppressed. It did not mean that they had to give their wealth to them, but they were required to share some of it. This was not considered charity but "justice." Even so, the Lord said that those who gave to the poor lent it to Him, and He would repay them. Jesus later said in His parable of the sheep and goats, that as we did anything for even the least of His people, it would be considered that we did it for Him. As one friend said, "The favor of God is worth a lifetime of effort," and taking care of those in need is one of the primary things that brought God's favor.

Some are poor because of their own irresponsibility, but many are locked in poverty because of things beyond their control, and it is right for us to help them. If we do not do what is our basic obligation, then the government has to do it, and it will not do it well. To even need a government safety net is evidence of the failure of religion in America. Both the Old and New Testaments call true religion taking care of the widows and orphans or the needy.

It is true that one negative action can overcome many positives, but the reverse is sometimes true also—one good deed can right many wrongs. If we have been blessed, regardless of how hard we worked for what we have, it is right to seek ways to use our blessings to help others who really need help.

Those who get engaged in true philanthropy learn quickly that to help one person rise above unfortunate circumstances can be more fulfilling than making many business deals. Besides the extraordinary satisfaction of this, it is right to be so engaged because it keeps us moored to the reality of this world, without which we will tend toward the ultimate evil of pride and self-righteousness. Helping the less fortunate was called "the obligation of the nobility" because we will lose true nobility if we are not personally engaged in helping others.

We will cover this in a bit more depth later, but let me reinforce the truth that the most effective antidote to Marxist foolishness is true justice. An aspect of true justice comes from the fortunate helping those less fortunate, voluntarily. Our government cannot give to anyone what it has not taken from someone else. Government largesse actually comes from what it has stolen from others, which is itself an injustice and will never be the basis for true justice. Thus, government charity almost never works and is usually counterproductive to really helping people.

Chapter Sixteen
FIXING HEALTHCARE

Providing quality, affordable healthcare for everyone is a noble goal, and it is achievable in America. Healthcare is not only one-sixth of the economy of America, but can profoundly impact the life of every single American. Our healthcare system is badly in need of some reforms. However, what was run through Congress and is now called Obamacare will not only destroy quality healthcare in America, it could destroy America.

Just the way that this legislation was run through Congress, without even giving those who had to vote on it the time to read and know what was in it, shocked millions of Americans. The good that this did was to wake up many more Americans to the present dysfunction of our government. When then Speaker of the House, Nancy Pelosi, made the statement that Congress should pass the bill so that they would then have time to read it and see what was in it, this revealed possibly more than anything ever could about just how broken and out of touch with reality our elected officials had become.

As America protested, possibly the most unpopular legislation in history was rammed down the throats of the American people. When the American people were told they just did not understand it, they became more incensed. The American people seem ready now to throw out anyone who treats them like ignorant children. Congress thought the public would have its typical short memory with this, but they didn't, getting more engaged for mid-term elections than possibly ever before. This is giving everyone, including business, the hope that out-of-control and out-of-touch government will be reined in. Even so, we must not throw out the truth that our healthcare system does need reform.

As Obamacare continues to get unpackaged, the shock effect grows as the provisions in it are revealed. Needed questions are starting to be asked: Who put those 2,700 pages together? Some of the most horrendous provisions in bills have been blamed on staffers slipping them in late at night. What could have possibly prevented this from happening in this bill? Aren't most of our elected officials lawyers, and isn't one of the first things taught in law school is that you never sign anything you do not read? How could they sign something that would so radically impact the future of the entire nation without reading it?

Why did they insist on doing it behind closed doors? President Obama promised openness and transparency in the process and to post each proposed bill on the Internet before passing it. In this case, even senators and congressmen were not given time to see what was in the bill before voting on it. Now we know why.

The Administration paid a high price for this at the polls in 2010. Even so, that the American people could be treated like this in the first place is incomprehensible. We must be sure that everyone responsible for this has to find a real job like the rest of us.

Under Obamacare, it will not take long to get to the place where it will be bureaucrats who will be deciding who gets medical help. This is as unfair to the bureaucrats as it will be for citizens. If you or a relative have ever suffered through treatment in a VA hospital, just consider that they are likely many times better than what our national healthcare system will be like if this legislation is not repealed. However, there is another way that will work faster and much better than any scenario yet presented to not only provide the best healthcare in the world, but at a fraction of what we are currently paying and at a fraction of what we will be paying if Obamacare is not repealed. Read on.

Good Medicine

Tort reform can fix almost all of the basic problems we have with our present healthcare system. It will make healthcare much better than it is now and cheaper! Tort reform would also provide a quick injection of trillions of dollars into the economy without adding more deficits. That is correct. Tort reform not only corrects the major problems in our healthcare, but will have a huge, positive impact on our entire economy. This could be as much of a positive infusion of cash as reducing government size to what it should be. How?

Presently, between 15% to 35% of the cost of major products, and a large and increasing percentage of the cost of every product in America, is for liability insurance. This is because of unrestrained and outrageously large damages awarded in lawsuits. Just placing reasonable caps on lawsuits would be one of the biggest and fastest boosts to our economy that could be made, putting this back into the hands of our people.

You cannot watch TV now without seeing ads to contact a law firm if you have taken a certain "bad drug." You are not only paying for that ad, but every time you see it, the price of drugs you buy in the future has probably gone up. Pharmaceutical firms have to build into the price of every drug they sell enough to pay for huge lawsuits that could hit them anytime in the future, even decades into the future. A side effect of a drug may not be discovered until it's been on the market for years or even decades, but the insurance companies covering the drug companies have to set aside for that provision now, so we have to pay for it now.

Let me relate a personal example of this. I owned an airplane more than twenty-five years ago that was recently involved in a crash. I was contacted by lawyers for a company that made just one of the dozens of instruments in this plane to ask me if I ever had any trouble with that relatively minor instrument. When I asked why they would even track me down to ask me such a question, they said it was because their company was being sued after the crash, even though the crash was obviously the result of pilot error. Every company who made any part for that plane was named in the suit and had to therefore defend themselves with expensive lawyers. They were included in the suit because the lawyers filing the suit knew most would settle for something out of court just to avoid the expense of going to court.

Think about every manufacturer now having to consider that just about anything they make today could result in them being named in a suit decades from now. They have to carry insurance for it now and will have to carry it for decades to come. Why would anyone even want to go into the business of manufacturing in America with such an unreal and unjust threat hanging over their heads? Fewer and fewer do, which is another reason why manufacturers are moving to other countries.

Why don't our politicians even talk about this? Because most of them are lawyers. Lawyers are virtually the only ones who are benefiting from the present warped state of affairs regarding lawsuits in America. Because suits are often appealed and take years to settle, the actual settlements are usually just enough to pay the lawyers—with the victims getting little or nothing. The present state of this in the U.S. is far outside the boundaries found in any other nation on earth, and it cannot last much longer here.

With the awakening now happening in America, there is rising hope that this too can finally be addressed. Fix this and many of the companies that would like to locate here, if it weren't for this, would come, bringing even more investment to America, not to mention creating a huge economic boom by putting so much more money back into the pockets of Americans, which is now going to ambulance chasers.

The fact that our present healthcare is so good and as cheap as it is, is the result of the genius of the free enterprise system as well as the great professionals in healthcare who do care. These have built the best healthcare system in the world despite almost impossible conditions allowed and promoted by the government. Presently, an increasing number of doctors have to stop practicing because they can no longer afford malpractice insurance.

The present Administration has tried to make us think that the insurance companies are the villains who are just raking it in at our expense, but they're not. Senate Majority Leader Harry Reid made a public statement that the profits of insurance companies had risen 400% the year before. This was 100 times the truth. The average profit margin of insurance companies was 4%. The highest was 6%. Their seemingly large increases were because they had made so little profit the year before that any increase seemed like a large jump.

One has to wonder why they even bother to go through all of the risk and hassles they do for such a small margin of profit. Then add to that the attacks they are suffering at the hands of their own government, and it seems as if the government is purposely trying to drive them out of the business. That would leave room for only one thing—the government option misnamed "public option." The Administration officials have been telling their base, which was insisting on a public option, that they will get the government option if they are just patient. That should make liberals happy unless they ever become a patient.

Tort reform could cut 30% or more off of healthcare costs immediately. Tort reform could also lead to relieving the burden of a mountain of unnecessary regulation that would save possibly as much again on healthcare costs. This would also free a lot of the time healthcare workers now have to spend on meaningless paperwork, as well as all they have to do to cover their backsides because of potential lawsuits. Maybe more importantly, it would free healthcare workers to use the most powerful medicine of all—hope. Few are willing to use this now, and have to be pessimistic about every prognosis for fear of a lawsuit if expectations are not met.

Tort reform would also free doctors to actually report problems and mistakes so that others could learn from them without having to make their own. This could save many lives each year. They cannot report mistakes now for fear of lawsuits, but making mistakes is a primary way we learn in order to improve medical procedures.

Tort reform would also cut out the majority of unnecessary and expensive testing because doctors no longer will feel they have to cover their behinds from every possible direction because of potential lawsuits. It has been estimated that up to 90% of tests are actually not necessary. If this figure is only half right, it would mean a huge savings for the entire country.

One good law that does need to be passed is that no healthcare worker should be able to receive commissions from tests they order. It's understandable now that doctors and workers need to make money to cover their huge malpractice insurance costs. We also need to remove this temptation to order unnecessary tests just for the profit by them.

Obviously, a large industry is now prospering because of these tests. People with special interests have learned to profit from the skewed system that is now in place and will fight every change. This is why strong, resolute leadership will be required for the times to come.

Think about this too—presently a doctor has to look at every patient as a potential adversary in court. Trust between doctor and patient is critical for healing, and this most basic need has been eroded because of the threat of a lawsuit.

There does need to be some recourse for negligence or mistakes that cause any patient harm. This is not to advocate eliminating malpractice suits, but only limiting awards and penalties to a reasonable amount, and eliminating frivolous ones. A part of tort reform should include capping the percentage of the settlement that is paid to lawyers to 15%. The costs of frivolous or baseless lawsuits should be borne by those making them, with a provision for them also paying the costs of those frivolously sued. This could be done in a way that does not discourage rightful suits but ensures that they are legitimate. Illegitimate suits are costing every American far more than most can even imagine. We are the ones paying for this present madness, and we are the ones who will have to correct it. To date we have not had elected officials with the courage to address this, though most of them know how bad it is.

The Clunker

Of course, allowing interstate competition between insurance companies could also help reduce insurance rates and further cut the cost of healthcare. Other major changes can and should be made to our healthcare system, but one we do not need is for the government to try to run it. Our government could not even run "Cash for Clunkers" well. For anyone to think the government is the best option for running something as complicated as healthcare is more than just Einstein's definition of insanity—it is a much higher form than that. For this law to have made it through Congress is shocking, but it reveals just how out of their minds our elected officials are right now.

"Cash for Clunkers" can tell us a lot about what government healthcare will be like. If you applied for cash as part of your clunker trade in, you had to fill out a 20-page contract! It should have been a single paragraph contract with just two questions: Is it a clunker? Who do you want the check made out to?

Then, do you remember when the first dealers tried to log in to apply for the "Cash for Clunkers" program and had to agree to conditions that made their computers and all of the contents in them government property? There was such an outcry that this requirement was dropped quickly, but we need to find out who put this in there and why.

Good Government Healthcare?

Now brace yourself for this thought—there is a way for the government to run healthcare and do it efficiently. That would require the most profound transformation of the present culture of our government to become efficient, but that is what must happen if we are going to make it through these times. When that has been accomplished, it is not out of the question that healthcare should be under either more government oversight or some degree of government management. Of course, right now it is hard to even compute that thought because government is so far from being able to do this.

I'm not saying this should be done even if the culture of government inefficiency was changed, but it could be done. If this culture of efficiency is restored to our government, it is not out of the question to think that the healthcare of the nation could to some degree be a part of our basic infrastructure available to all citizens and legal guests in the nation. Just a thought.

Proponents of Obamacare are arguing now that they are going to run the system effectively and efficiently, but until we have even one good example of the government ever doing this, we are the biggest of all fools to believe them. Until a culture of efficiency is established and proven in government, government-run healthcare is one of the most frightening threats we're facing as a nation.

Because of how easily and fast government programs get politicized, it is likely to always be far too dangerous to ever consider a government-run healthcare system anyway. Even so, serious pros and cons should at least be considered, but only after government makes a radical change to be efficient and effective.

The key words in the previous paragraph are "radical change." Radical means basic, and this is one of the ultimate answers to just about everything that ails us at this time—we have departed from the basics. The most successful people in virtually every field are those who do the basics best. The basics that were the foundation of the United States are the basis of our success, strength, and prosperity. We have run into our greatest troubles when we have drifted from them. Most of the solutions to our greatest problems are found in returning to the basics of our Constitution and Bill of Rights, which had their roots in a strong Judeo/Christian moral compass.

CHAPTER SEVENTEEN
BUILDING BRIDGES

America's infrastructure is in desperate need of repair. When the bridge that thousands crossed every day going into Minneapolis collapsed, everyone in America started being concerned about the bridges they have to cross. They should be. The physical infrastructure of America is in need of restoration and renewal, just like the heart and soul of America. For a time, the collapsed bridge going into Minneapolis became a symbol of the needed restoration in America, and it was a good one. We need a renewed vision and purpose, a bridge into the future that can safely carry the weight of our purpose.

I once heard a wise preacher say that all relationships are built on trust. You can like someone, and even love them, but if you do not trust that person, you cannot have much of a relationship. Trust is the bridge between people, and the amount of weight that can be carried across that bridge depends on how much trust there is.

America is presently in a period of profound and growing distrust in its own government. This is the result of disillusionment, which is a good thing—when you are disillusioned, you are losing your illusions. We have had illusions about our government, but now we're starting to see it the way that it really is. It is not likely this generation of Americans will be so easily fooled again. However, we must not stay in this place of distrust, but rather work to rebuild a government that can be trusted. This needs to begin by having a government and leaders within who tell us the truth. Then we need them to be proven and trustworthy stewards of what we are entrusting to them.

Because we are now in a time when our trust in government is going down fast, we can expect Americans to challenge future leaders on an unprecedented level before giving them their trust. That is the way it should be, and it can help lead us to a much more stable future if we will maintain this healthy skepticism. If trust in our government is to be rebuilt, it must be by the government becoming trustworthy again.

Trust Your Eyes

There was once a cartoon of a dictator saying to the people, "Are you going to trust what you see with your eyes, or what I tell you?" Many would apply this now to our own news media. The erosion of trust in the media has been just about as deep as the erosion of trust in government. Only a couple of decades ago Americans tended to believe just about anything they heard on the news. Now the opposite is true—they doubt just about anything they get from the news media.

This is encouraging in some ways because Americans are becoming far more educated and knowledgeable of current events. However, it is discouraging that our news media has fallen so low, become so political, and is no longer worthy of our trust. Freedom requires trustworthy information, and there is an increasing need for trustworthy news sources at this time.

There is healthy skepticism and unhealthy skepticism. The healthy kind wants to believe but will check out everything thoroughly before doing so. The unhealthy kind does not want to believe and will usually only acknowledge what it wants to believe. In general, Americans are healthy with their skepticism—they want to believe, but you had better have the goods. However, cynicism has been growing, and this is not healthy. There is a difference between wise judgment and the cynicism that sees everything from the dark side.

To trust our government is good if it is trustworthy, but even then it needs to be thoroughly and continually examined. We have been putting too much trust in government to solve all of our problems, and now we're waking up to the fact that it is causing them. This is healthy because it is the truth. Until recently, we could trust the news media to do the investigating, and we could trust their reports. Now journalists have fallen off of the charts of trusted professionals, even falling below preachers and lawyers!

It is a good thing that Americans are now beginning to demand substance behind what they are going to accept and who they are going to trust. This was a basic quality that the Founding Fathers thought citizens of a republic needed in order for the republic to survive. Our Founding Fathers did not trust government very much, even the one they created. They already recognized what Lord Acton would state so succinctly one hundred years later: "Power tends to corrupt, and absolute power corrupts absolutely." For this reason, they devised a system that would restrain the ambitions of those seeking power over the people in order to ensure that the people would have power over their government.

America has drifted from that wisdom and has allowed the power of government over the people to be increased. Now the power of the people to check government's increasingly domineering and controlling ways has been eroded. Some administrations may have slowed this drift, but at best, they have only slowed it. We may be at the very end of the window of opportunity for reversing this. The good thing is that much of America is now waking up and is willing to do what it takes to reverse this.

Relevant and Effective Government

No doubt the world in which we now live is very different from the world of our Founding Fathers. However, the government they devised was one that could be relevant and effective in any age because it was not structured to just relate to the times, but to relate to the basic, proven nature of people. That nature has not changed since their time, and the government they devised to compensate for it remains the most remarkable, brilliant, and effective government ever devised for the human race.

Many believe government is the answer to all of our problems and will argue that in this increasingly modern and dangerous world we need more government control. However, the reverse is actually true. It is true that government can and must do some things that the private citizens or the private sector will never be able to do, such as providing national defense and being the referee in commerce it is supposed to be. However, its ability to do those things is eroded when it wastes its attention and resources in areas it should not be managing, therefore trying to do things it cannot do well. We need a strong, efficient, effective government, but only in the areas where it has been proven trustworthy and capable.

Hitting "Reset"

You can have the best form of government but still have bad government if you have bad people in it. Likewise, you can have a poor form of government but have good government if you have good people in it. Even so, the best of all would be to have a good form of government and good people in it. Our form of government is not perfect, but it has proven to be the best ever devised. It is up to us to ensure that good people are in it.

The process that has evolved for choosing our leaders and representatives has become one that attracts many with less than honorable intentions and repels those who would likely be the best leaders and representatives. One encouraging trend has been the town hall meetings, the Tea Party gatherings, and other events that reveal a great awakening among the American people. There is a movement to insist on better leaders and representatives. If this continues, there is great hope for the future of America.

The kind of in-your-face challenges many representatives got from their constituents when they held town hall meetings in 2009 was a shock to them. Then as a shock to the people, the representatives went back to Washington and opposed the obvious will of the people so blatantly by passing the healthcare reform bill anyway. Worse still, they did it by a process that was intended to hide what they were doing, and the things they were putting in this bill, from the American people. Most encouragingly the American people did not lie down, but carried their outrage to the polls in 2010. That was a start, but we cannot stop there.

The results of this mid-term election have rightly given the people hope, but the war to retake our government and make it "of the people, by the people, and for the people" again has not been won. Even so, what we are now seeing rising in America could be the beginning of a second American Revolution that recovers what was won by the first one.

As stated, another encouraging trend is that there are strong indications that Americans are returning to their historic roots, evidenced by the way books on the Founding Fathers, the Constitution, the Bill of Rights, and our early history are rising on the bestselling lists. I do not remember a time like now when you could hear so many conversations from citizens about how certain things being proposed by the government violate the Constitution, while they are citing the chapter and verse in the Constitution that is being violated. Many of our politicians and much of the news media are still treating Americans as if they are ignorant, but the media is doing this at its own peril.

Barring a major national catastrophe, America seems to be righting itself, getting back to its solid foundation, with a great resolve to fasten herself more firmly to it so this does not happen again.

CHAPTER EIGHTEEN
TRAUMA REVEALS

Trauma can sharpen judgment, or it can blur it more than just about anything else, depending on how we react to it. In the past, trauma has tended to sharpen and focus the better traits of Americans, but this may be the result of the extraordinary leadership we've seemed to always be blessed with in such times.

Having studied leadership for over thirty years, I've discovered that one who is a good leader through trauma may not be a good one in peacetime, and vice versa. With the rising tensions and crises in the world and in our own country, we need leadership that can function well under pressure. These leaders are not common. One of the most important questions we can ask: How can we attract such as these to government where they are so desperately needed at this time?

The best crisis leaders are devoted to truth and integrity, and display strong moral convictions, and often strong spiritual convictions. That's not just my opinion. Good leaders have been driven by a noble purpose, not by selfish ambition which is so demeaning.

As touched on before, as a flight instructor, and for a time a pilot examiner, one of the main things I learned to evaluate in pilots was their ability to cope with emergencies. Once you've learned to take off, fly straight and level, turn, descend, and land, almost all of your training and testing revolved around dealing with emergencies. The real skills and judgment of a pilot were revealed during an emergency far more than in any other phase of flight. National crises likewise reveal possibly more about a country, its people, and its leaders than anything else.

Crisis Character

Crises can also change you faster and more radically than possibly anything. There have been two great crises in America over the last few years that have revealed much about us and have fashioned us into who we now are in some ways. One was the attack on 9/11 and the other was Hurricane Katrina. There have been many other crises, including the economic crises, which also reveal a lot about us, but 9/11 and Katrina were particularly illuminating.

Our church got engaged in the disaster response after Hurricane Katrina. Teams from our churches and schools rotated to the distribution base we built in Biloxi, Mississippi. Our school kids said they got more education in a week there than they might get in school in a year. No doubt the best and worst in people were revealed in that crisis, but in some ways possibly the best and worst in the nation too.

We were there almost before the hurricane winds stopped blowing, and stayed for four months. Our base was at what was probably the most devastated part of the region. We saw the good, the bad, and the ugly, and there was a lot of each. After the whole experience, I have never been more proud to be an American, or more concerned about America. It became obvious to me there that if the fundamental core of our government and the direction we were headed as a nation was not changed, we would become increasingly vulnerable during crises. To date, neither the core of our government nor the direction of the nation has changed, at least not the way we need to in order to cope with the times.

We saw the worst of just about everything, but we never saw any racism on the part of any Federal government official and never heard of any from a reliable source. It was the opposite, and

I became very thankful for a government that cared as much as it did for its people and that would try so hard to help them when in need. Nevertheless, I was just as shocked by the incompetence of our government, with the exception of the Army. When the Army showed up things got done, bottlenecks were broken through, and the lawlessness that had broken out was quickly brought under control.

On the other hand, there was a lot of obvious racism on the part of some local government officials who made accusations in order to deflect attention away from their own incompetence and failures in the crisis. For them to blame the Federal government was the worst kind of hypocrisy, but they got away with it without being challenged. The failures of the Federal government were not racial but the result of red tape and regulations that had emergency workers so tied up they could not move with the agility this crisis demanded.

There were many examples of how our government was too encumbered by overregulation or ridiculous regulations to effectively deal with this crisis. One that stands out as typical was when a FEMA fuel truck showed up to provide for the emergency vehicles in Slidell, Louisiana. Because these emergency vehicles did not have the FEMA-approved receptacles, the fuel truck drove away without giving them any fuel. People were dying at that time. The mayor responded like a hero and ordered his people to go to the airport and drain the airplanes of their fuel. He knew that aviation fuel would eventually burn up the engines, but they would work long enough to save some.

When President Bush came down, he quickly saw the problems and immediately gave orders to FEMA that helped break through the bottlenecks and started getting resources to the needs. He too was one of the heroes of Katrina to those who were actually there. Because the media used the crisis as an opening to jump on him, and said little or nothing about the real culprits, what was reported was often very different from what was actually being seen by those on the ground. Those in such crisis situations usually learn very fast how skewed our media can be. When I visited the Gulf Coast after the BP oil spill disaster, it was obvious that this had not changed. The Administration's response and leadership, or lack of it, was far worse in the BP disaster than at Katrina, but you could not learn this from the media.

In the Katrina crisis, the day was saved mostly by the people of America who showed up in their pickup trucks filled with bottled water, food, and clothes. Corporations sent their corporate planes loaded with provisions, and their trucks came down loaded with tents, clothes, and other provisions. It was wonderful to see the people, churches, synagogues, mosques, and companies who responded to this. I was never more alarmed at the incompetence, ineffectiveness, and inefficiency of the most wealthy, powerful government in the world. I remain alarmed that the real causes of this incompetence have still not been addressed.

We do not have competent crisis leadership and good basic crisis planning, and we need them immediately with all of the potential threats we're facing. Certainly there are exceptions to this on local levels, and FEMA has done great in some crises, but overall we are exposed and unprepared for major crises that don't fit into our expectations. This is one of the desperate needs we have at this time because great and unusual crises are becoming the norm, not the exception. We need a leadership who can think and be proactive in completely unusual situations, even in chaos, and bring order out of it.

Are We Beasts?

When the lights went out in New York City, people became like beasts with their pillaging and plundering, causing the Prime Minister of Britain at the time, Margaret Thatcher, to remark, "The veneer of civilization is very thin." In a crisis like Katrina that lasts for an extended time, this can be a much greater problem. This reveals that lawlessness, not order, is in the hearts of many and will surface in a crisis.

I quit counting how many hurricanes I've been through personally. Each one is a disaster, and after the first ones I started to see a pattern. For about the first 24 to 48 hours, people were so happy just to be alive that they tend to be abnormally gracious. After that, fear starts to set in because of the huge mess. This may last for a day or two. Then it turns into anger and then rage.

The combination of fear and anger can be powerful and can contribute significantly to the problems everyone is facing. The worse the damage or crisis, the faster and more profound these trends tend to manifest. We can be more prepared for this if we understand it, so we will go a little deeper into the causes.

A Root of Lawlessness

A couple of weeks into the Katrina crisis, I sat in a mess tent with some of our workers. One of them pointed out to me how they could quickly tell which hurricane victims had been living on entitlements and which ones worked for a living. They pointed to a rather small African-American man who they said lost his family and everything he owned. He was obviously dealing with unimaginable grief, but whenever a truck pulled in, or there was something to do at the base, he was always one of the first to offer to help, and would help, working very hard. There were others there who had suffered unimaginable loss too, but they too were always ready to help when there was something to be done. It was just their nature. All of these worked for a living.

Those who lived on welfare were different. Not only were they outrageously demanding, they would get angry if they were asked to do something, even a small thing. We had high school and college students who volunteered to be there and were obviously doing it at great risk and working harder than they ever had in their lives for many hours a day. Some of those who had been on welfare would get in the face of these kids at times, demanding to be served and taken care of, often for things they should easily have been able to do themselves. It seemed that right on our base we had both the best and worst of humanity. One basic contrast separated them—working for a living or living on welfare.

Call this profiling, but there is some profiling that everyone does. What we're talking about here is not a racial factor—it's an entitlement factor. The entitlement mentality we have allowed has turned some who might otherwise be some of the best people into some of the worst. The blame for this is squarely on us for allowing our government to do it to them.

One time the administrator of our K-12 private school came to me with a very interesting observation. In any school you will always have problem parents who want to blame others for their children's problems, and this is just one of the things you learn to deal with. However, that year it was noted that every single parent who was like this had children we were giving aid or scholarships to. Not a single parent who paid regular tuition was one of these complainers. You would think it would be the opposite, but when I started checking other years, and throughout other departments in the church and ministries we had, it was universal; those who received aid were inevitably the most demanding.

After Katrina, we brought some of the victims to North Carolina, gave them places to live, and tried to find them jobs. The shock came when some became offended when we tried to get them jobs. They thought that we should just keep on supporting them. These were rather young, able-bodied, and smart. When one couple was caught selling drugs, they became outraged and threatening when we told them we were not going to support them any longer. I don't even remember being thanked by anyone living on entitlements for the things we did for them, even when we did it at great personal risk and expense. The gratitude from those who worked for a living made it all worth it many times over, but we really need to understand just how potentially dangerous the entitlement mentality is.

These are anecdotes, not scientific studies. Maybe no one wants to do such impact studies on entitlements because you have to tread so close to profiling. Profiling can be a terrible thing for our minority citizens. I've had many friends who were African-American, professional athletes, and know the struggles they had deciding whether to buy the kind of car they wanted, and could well afford, but a African-American man or woman in an expensive car is subject to constant police stops. Our Hispanic citizens are likewise subject to increasing profiling in these times regardless of how long their families have been Americans. We should be thankful that our country is sensitive to profiling, but profiling is a fact of life, and it happens all of the time by everyone. Few things so skew accurate knowledge, wisdom, and understanding than the oversensitivity to profiling now promoted as political correctness. The key word here is "oversensitivity." It is actually making us almost powerless against some of the greatest threats we face, including terrorism.

The Deception of Political Correctness

The well-publicized strategy of Islamic jihadists to bring down America is to use our own Constitution, relativism, and political correctness against us. The results of this irrational fear of social profiling, fueled by extreme political correctness, is well revealed in the 2009 Department of Homeland Security (DHS) memo about groups that were potential domestic terrorist threats. It listed Christians, Amendment Two advocates, and veterans as potential terrorist threats. The first thing we need to ask is: Isn't that social profiling? Why didn't the media call their hand on that one?

To show how demented our thinking can get with an over-devotion to political correctness, this memo did not even mention the one group that has been the source of over 99% of all terrorist attacks throughout the world over the last half century—Islamic jihadists! When was the last time there was a Christian suicide bomber or Amendment Two advocate who flew planes into buildings?

Could there be a more dramatic example of how demented some people get from a devotion to political correctness? This came from our own DHS—the ones most responsible for our protection.

Our DHS then boasted about the thwarted Christmas Day "crotch bomber" and the failed attempted bombing at Times Square, saying "the system worked." If it worked, how did the crotch bomber get on the plane? Did DHS stop the Times Square bomber? This attack was foiled by a hot dog vendor!

Reason should make us more inclined to spend the billions now being given to DHS to hire hot dog vendors to protect our cities. This would not only make us safer, it would help with the unemployment problem. By the way, the hot dog vendor was a veteran that the DHS has made clear it is more worried about than the Muslim bomber. They cannot view a Muslim as a terrorist threat because that would be profiling, but they can view Christians as threats. Go figure. This is the United States of America where 80% of the citizens claim to be Christians!

Remember a few chapters back we discussed how an action in one area of a process can have quite unexpected and extreme consequences down the line in the process? How could a U.S. Army major, an officer who swore to defend the Constitution from enemies both foreign and domestic, not be investigated after making speeches to his fellow officers about the justice of killing American soldiers in Iraq?

What kind of political dementia would have the U.S. Army Chief of Staff, whose own soldiers were lying dead all over the floor in the supposed security of their own fort on home soil, say almost before their bodies had been picked up that he was more concerned about "diversity being wounded"? We should all appreciate the diversity of our culture, but this is how one of the top officers responsible for our defense was thinking, and that is scary. When you're dead, diversity does not matter very much.

The jihadists' strategy of using political correctness against us has worked brilliantly, probably far more than they ever dreamed. It has caused us to lower our guard against terrorists whose whole intent is to destroy us, and like the 9/11 terrorists many of them are living among us and seem like such nice people. As one of the basic principles of warfare states, you cannot defeat an enemy you do not recognize, and we have been blinded by political correctness so that we cannot see.

It may seem extreme now, but the entitlement mentality we have sown into so many is a time bomb, and it can rise up to be one of the greatest threats to our domestic security. Not only will these be prone to riot when they do not get their way, but they will be a seedbed for terrorism.

The good thing is that many Americans who are losing trust in their government and in the media are becoming much more resourceful. Many are starting to learn all that they can about taking care of their families in a crisis and how to get their own accurate information. Because so many Americans are starting to get involved, there is a very good reason to trust that we have a future and a bright one—Americans are amazing and resourceful people who will find a way to prevail.

When our government is again "of the people, by the people, and for the people," we will have great government again too. The public's low esteem of the media for so twisting the truth will one day also result in a media we can trust again. However, as trustworthy as both the government and the media could one day be, and as competent as they might yet become, we cannot lose our own resourcefulness.

Chapter Nineteen
SEEING THE FUTURE

A merica was founded and established by men and women of great national vision and purpose. This was a vision of freedom so strong that they were willing to fight the most powerful empire in the world to achieve it. In the Declaration of Independence the signers wrote, "With a firm reliance on the protection of divine Providence, we mutually pledge to each other our Lives, our Fortunes, and our sacred Honor." These were not empty words! They would immediately be hunted down as traitors and hung for treason if caught. Some paid the ultimate price. Two of the signers, who were very wealthy, would immediately lose everything they had when they signed because British forces were camped next to their estates. They signed anyway.

For more than two hundred years, millions of other Americans have arisen to face the greatest threats to their country and willingly paid the ultimate price. Facing the ultimate threats of Nazism and Japanese Imperialism, America stood and fought until victory was complete. Then without time to even catch their breath, they stood fast against communism without flinching and prevailed. The root of the struggle has always been about freedom, and every generation has proven willing to sacrifice their lives, their fortunes, and their sacred honor in order to preserve it.

Between the continuous challenges to America's very existence, no breaks were taken, but a great and powerful nation was built. It is in our national DNA to be explorers, pioneers, innovators, and inventors. We are a nation that will not do well without national vision and purpose, always challenging the present limits of the times.

Where does this remarkable energy come from? Vision and a noble purpose. Vision is what imparts the energy necessary for accomplishment. To provide well for our families is a noble goal, but to be truly noble, we must provide our families with more than stuff—they need to know the obligation that comes with wealth and power to use it for good.

Some recent studies on happiness are very interesting and revealing. The researchers found one basic factor to be the most common and enduring foundation of happiness that no one doing the study was expecting to find—a simple life. Another factor the researchers were not expecting to find about happiness was that it seemed to have no connection to possessions. Poor people tended to be much happier than those who had much more. Because their lives were simpler, the poor tended to put more value on the one common denominator that all happy people had—strong relationships.

Of course, there are exceptions to this interesting finding about the most common factor for happiness. There are wealthy people with a lot of stuff who are happy too. There are also many poor who are bitter and disgruntled people. Why can't we have a vision for being wealthy, which we are as a nation, but keep our lives simple enough to esteem and give ourselves to the relationships that are the foundation of true happiness, using our wealth to invest in people?

Jesus taught that we should make friends with money. He did not mean that we should make money our friend, but that we should use money to make friends with—use it to invest in people. This is actually the motive behind the foreign aid America gives to other nations. However, at present, this is often managed like the government manages everything else, very poorly. Far too often our aid only ends up in the coffers of some evil leaders who are oppressing their people, and it only promotes an entitlement mentality in them. Even so, the principle is right even if the application is done poorly. When our own house is in order again, America should be willing to help other nations, but in a way that really helps them.

Giving Capitalism a Good Name

As discussed earlier, at the top of the list of the richest people in the world are Bill Gates and Warren Buffett. Both Gates and Buffett decided to give almost their entire fortunes into a trust that would be used to help others. This astonished everyone who heard it, and it is certainly a remarkable and noble deed for them to do this, but it is also the type of generosity sown into the original DNA of America. America loves to achieve, and then we love to share the fruits of our achievements.

In the Gospels, there is a story of a rich young ruler who came to Jesus and declared that he kept all of the commandments. He asked what else he needed to do to inherit eternal life. Jesus told him to give his possessions to the poor and come and follow Him. Because he had so much, this rich young ruler just could not do it. Others have.

In the 1700s, there was a young German Count who was obviously one of the richest men in the world at the time. He was reported to have died penniless but also as one of the happiest men in the world. He was happy because he had expended his entire fortune sending missionaries to preach the gospel to some of the poorest people on earth. Historians call him the rich young ruler who said "yes." His legacy? He was the true father of modern missions, which even William Carey, who is often called the father of modern missions, acknowledged to have been his own inspiration. He also may be the one person most responsible for setting the spiritual genetic code of America. This man who imparted a higher standard of nobility throughout Western civilization was Count Ludwig von Zinzendorf.

In the 1750s, Count Zinzendorf established a base in what is now Bethlehem, Pennsylvania and another in what is now Winston-Salem, North Carolina. These bases were to be used for reaching the American people with the gospel and to especially help the Indians. In North Carolina, he named the one-hundred-thousand-acre track he purchased, "The Wachovia Track." Wachovia means "a bountiful field," which was certainly what America was to become. I am writing this from a porch on the western edge of the land purchased by this truly noble Count.

Zinzendorf was a significant inspiration to those who were to have the greatest impact on that remarkable century in America, Europe, and virtually all of the new nations that were being born at the time. The people and places where he had the most impact seem to all be marked, not only by commercial prosperity, but also by a remarkable generosity of spirit. This generous spirit is a basic part of the spirit of America where Zinzendorf has such a legacy. Americans are generous by nature, and we become unhappy, and at times very bad, when we become greedy and selfish.

There can be a difference between riches and wealth. In the Book of Proverbs, we are told that riches come fast but makes wings for itself, meaning it will likely disappear just as fast as it came (see Proverbs 23:5). Wealth has depth and longevity, which can be passed on for generations. Riches come from things like winning the lottery. Wealth is built with patience, hard work, endurance, and the wisdom that comes from many trials. Therefore, wealth has roots and tends to grow instead of shrink.

America has wealth, not just riches. Our wealth is not measured just in our dollars or our property, but it is the fabric of who we are as a nation—a people with great initiative and good tendencies.

Certainly America has been through less than noble times, deeds, and people, which it is good to remember and be humbled by. We do need to be vigilant against the evil and the greed because it always costs us dearly. However, the biggest inroad for evil seems to be when the good cease to be proactive and engaged, devoted to doing good, and so the vacuum is filled by those with less than noble motives.

I know a number of wealthy people. Most think and talk a lot about how to do good for others. However, most of these don't know how to do the good they would like to do. They see the inefficiency and waste in charities and ministries and the lack of good management that causes them to not want to invest in them. Even so, Americans are today the most generous people in the world and could be even more so if there were more efficient, effective outlets.

Poor management is sometimes just as much of a problem with large charities as it is with government. Most charities cannot pay wages comparable to the private sector and thus may not be able to attract great managers. Poor management is an almost universal problem outside of business and sometimes in business too. With all of the wealth we have been made stewards of, we have a responsibility to learn how to manage it well.

As you certainly know by now, a basic theme of this book is how better management of our resources is the answer to some of our biggest problems. As we discussed, the road to hell can be paved with good intentions. Good intentions can help good things get started, and we should be thankful for the good intentions, but add to them good stewardship of the resources so that real help and real change are possible.

The Facts

Government cannot give to anyone what it has not taken from someone else. It does not get its resources from producing or marketing anything, but from taking taxes from the people. For the basic responsibilities our Founding Fathers gave the Federal government the mandate to do, such as defense and regulating interstate commerce, most Americans would think they get a good deal for what they are charged in taxes. It's in the things that the

Federal government was never mandated to do that the waste, inefficiency, and incompetence becomes intolerable.

Even though we do get a lot for our taxes, they are now growing so exorbitant that we are beginning to eat our seed, and our future is being quickly consumed. This is unnecessary because so much is just being wasted by poor management. The people are now starting to rebel and demand change. We can expect movements like the Tea Party to keep growing until this is corrected. If the government would stick to what it can do well, and stay out of what it can't do well, our taxes would be a fraction of what they are now.

Presently, as much as 90% of any money that passes through government is consumed by bureaucracy and red tape. That is correct—as little as 10% actually gets out the other side and makes it to the needs. The opposite should be the case where 90% makes it to the designated purpose and only 10% is used for program administration. With the automation we have today, it could easily be accomplished.

Cold Love

Another problem we have with government social programs is that when charity becomes institutional, it becomes cold and demeaning. Institutional charity also tends to just feed the entitlement mentality rather than being used to help people get back on their own feet. The new breed of minority leadership that is now rising knows this, and they do not want charity for their people—they want opportunity. They don't want schools that pander to and pass everyone—they want them to be educated so they can have a real chance to be successful in life. The new breed is calling welfare what it is—slavery in another form, and they are determined to throw this yoke off. We need to help them.

How do we get there from here? It will not be easy, but it will be worth it. It needs to be done with patience and understanding. Many people have been conditioned by their circumstances, and it takes time to change this conditioning, but it can be done. When it is done, everyone will be happier and much better off. Let's look at just a couple of the major factors we must overcome to bring this desperately needed change in our country.

Broken Decision Maker

If someone has been in prison for very long, his or her "decision maker" becomes atrophied. After a few years, this gets to the point where a prisoner cannot make even a basic decision for themselves such as going to the toilet without getting permission. I have seen a number of people get out of prison who could not make decisions like choosing from a menu without great turmoil. This is why many prisoners who are released end up committing crimes to purposely get caught so that they can go back to prison. In prison, they feel more secure because all of their decisions are being made for them, and they can no longer do this for themselves.

This is also why so many who lived under communism wanted to return to communism after tasting freedom for just a little while. Those who had been in the prison of communism for so long could not quickly start functioning in freedom—they needed someone to make decisions for them. This is also why the children of Israel led by Moses wanted to return to Egypt after experiencing just a little freedom. Israel got out of Egypt in one night, but it took forty years to get the Egyptian slave mentality out of them. It would need to be a new generation that could function in their Promised Land with liberty.

People who have lived by entitlements for long, who have others providing for them and making most of their life decisions for them, are likewise going to need time to rebuild their own initiative and be able to cope with freedom, much less enjoy it. So charity, or welfare reform, will take some time if done right. It must not be reduced to just providing needs more efficiently; it must also start to help elevate the people being helped. Studies have shown that people will go insane if they are deprived of meaningful labor, and there is a form of insanity that comes upon those who are not engaged in producing something. We have to help people get off of welfare for their sakes, not just to save money.

This was a part of the philosophy behind President George W. Bush's "Faith Based Initiative." This program may have had some flaws, but it was a step in the right direction—to get the aid people needed flowing through caring people rather than a cold, hard bureaucracy. This program was modeled after some amazing success stories, some of which I was able to personally witness and be a small part of. This initiative was started by a group of NFL and NBA players who wanted to help their families and communities, but who had witnessed how destructive just giving them money could be.

Building People

For several years, I worked with Reggie White, the former NFL great, who developed a successful aid program called The Society of Nehemiah Project. Reggie was one of the most dominating defensive linemen to ever play the game, and at six foot six and over three hundred pounds of almost pure muscle, he was a terror to every opposing quarterback. Off the field, I don't think I ever met a more compassionate person whose heart seemed even bigger than his huge body. For years, we talked on the phone almost every night. I remember him calling me right after some of the biggest playoff games of his career, and he would not even mention football, but instead wanted to talk about a plan he had for helping someone.

Most of the other professional athletes I've known were also devoted to helping the less fortunate. The news tends to highlight the mistakes of sports heroes, but in general, professional athletes must have uncommon vision, focus, and discipline to play on the professional level in any sport, and they also want to be a blessing to their communities.

Professional athletes almost all share a big problem—everyone wants their money. Most are constantly bombarded with requests for loans or gifts by relatives and friends. Most of these athletes learn fast that giving people money rarely helps them, and that they are just throwing their money away if they give it to them. Many are criticized for leaving their poor neighborhoods and not returning, but there is no way for them to return without constant pressure from those who want their money—and actually feel entitled to it.

It was rare to walk through a public place with Reggie without someone coming up to him and asking for money. Reggie was one of the most highly visible and most interviewed people in the league when he played, and I remember one shoeshine man spotting him and running over to ask Reggie for a loan of $50,000. Most of those people would get angry when Reggie would not do it, even wanting him to write them a check on the spot.

Reggie wanted to help people and really felt that his blessing was for that purpose, but he did not know how to do it. He had made many loans to people, and he confided in me once that he did not know of a single one that really helped anyone. Almost all lost it fast, and they would then be back for more. Finally, Reggie thought of a way he would not have to say "no" to people but also would not have the money squandered. This is how The Society of Nehemiah began.

Reggie and his wife Sarah developed a program where anyone seeking a loan would go through classes to learn the basics of business—like writing a business plan, building a team, basic management, and so forth. Then the classes would break up into accountability groups and vote on the best plans that would get a grant. As soon as that business was successful, they would meet to help the next one get going. It worked brilliantly.

As stated earlier, about 75% of all start-up businesses fail in the first year, and almost 90% will be gone in less than 2 years. The businesses started through The Society of Nehemiah had a success rate of over 95%. They were all small start-ups, as they needed to be so that the owners could grow in wisdom and knowledge as their businesses grew. Some did grow to be quite large. They had a good foundation; they had mentors; and they had accountability. It was a lot of work, but people are worth it, and true success requires it.

There was more to The Society of Nehemiah than this, but it was used to start many successful small businesses, and it became an inspiration for The Faith Based Initiative. When these ideas passed through government, they got changed, but if the core principles are reapplied, they will work and could help reduce the government burden of welfare.

The burden of welfare now placed on government can be lifted. This is not just visionary but doable. We do not need to deprive those who are counting on Social Security and Medicaid of what they are expecting. In fact, we could do more for people than they're expecting if all of these programs were run as efficiently as they should be. America could also get weaned off of these programs in a very efficient, orderly, and humane way.

Lasting Success

The true wealth of America is not measured just in dollars or GDP, but in the initiative, resolve, endurance, wisdom, faith, and knowledge of Americans. Success cannot be defined by how much we have but by what we become. America has generous natural resources, but the powerful economic engine America became was not the result of these—our economic engine runs on vision and ingenuity. America had this ingenuity because of the freedom that set the human soul free to create. These grew with the stability of a government based on a Constitution and Bill of Rights that were written with great and unprecedented genius for government.

The root of every major crisis now besetting America can be directly traced to a departure from the wisdom of this great foundation laid by our Founding Fathers. The way out of these crises is to return to these wise and practical ways that will elevate and free those who live by them. They were unique when developed, and they remain unique in many ways, setting the course of a government that did not control and use the people, but set them free and served them.

The freed human spirit can do what no government has ever done or can do. It was in America that it was first proposed that the people did not exist for the government, but the government existed for the people—to provide the security and conditions for releasing the human spirit to be what it was created to be. For the first time in history, the government was seen as the servant of the people, not their master. It was because of this radical new precept that the greatest advance of civilization in history was released. It can be released again, and we can go higher.

In a republic, it is up to the people to demand quality leadership and management of their government. Again, "If you do not change your direction, you will end up where you are headed." Where we've been headed in recent times is a place we do not want to go, and so we must change our direction. It is up to us to stand up and demand real change. There is a mobilization beginning now—become a part of it.

We have everything we need to achieve on the list in the first chapter—except the leadership in place with the vision and resolve to do it. The core values, beliefs, and resolve that founded America, that propelled it to becoming the greatest nation in history, are still the core values of the majority of Americans. We can be greater still. The choice is ours.

The Exception

Again, the term "American exceptionalism" is not arrogance, but true. There has been no other nation in history like the United States. We are an exception in many ways, and these exceptions have proven to release people to be what we were created to be. Our freedom is an offense to many who are still in prison nations, and we are a challenge even to those who have some freedom. This challenge is a good thing and can help set many others free as well. Understanding how and why we are different, and having the courage to be different, are keys to understanding and releasing the future potential of America.

163

Because of the unique history and present makeup of America, there would no doubt be serious violence if the kinds of restraints were imposed on America that other nations seem comfortable with. When the present Administration tried to jerk America hard toward socialism, America jerked back harder. At this writing, there is a strong national resolve to move back to her center-right bearings. There is a danger that the shock of what the Administration tried to do may cause us to overreact for a time and move even further right than we may need to do. Even so, America will find her way right back to where her heart of hearts tells her she should be.

Where is that? If you would take a scale of 1 to 10, with one being extreme left and ten being the extreme right, America is about a 6—just a little center-right. Americans want a strong government, but we don't want too much of it. We want freedom but also with the responsibility of taking care of those who truly need help.

Virtually everyone is waking up to how tragically inefficient and poorly managed government is and how so little of the resources dedicated to the needy gets to them. Even so, many would still rather have the government do this because they do not want to be bothered by it. However, there is another way, and a much better one.

This job needs to be given to those who really want to do it. They may need to be trained to manage the job more efficiently, and they must be held accountable for how they manage our resources devoted to this. However, those who have a heart to do it will have the possibility of doing it right.

CHAPTER TWENTY

FROM MANY ONE

The word "university" came from the idea of "unity in diversity." America is like a university of the nations. We are made up of immigrants from all nations, and we draw from the strength of them all. For this reason, immigration has also been a foundational strength of America that keeps her renewed.

There is always a challenge to incorporating new groups, or new ideas, but if you can do it, the benefits are great. Christ taught that you cannot put new wine in an old wineskin because new wine requires a vessel that is flexible and expandable. Bringing new people groups into America has constantly stretched us, enabling us to remain flexible and expandable to incorporate new ideas. To have a country that values traditions and history, while also embracing the new with such enthusiasm, is not common.

Immigration—the Hot Potato

Now immigration is a major issue, with a number of sub-issues attached that are also major. Presently, it is estimated that 12 million to 20 million illegal immigrants are living in the United States. This is a dominant issue now and has the potential of ratcheting up dramatically to become even more serious. Like most of our other crises, the longer we delay in addressing it, the harder it will be to fix.

Our borders must be secured, and entry by illegal means must be stopped. That is not negotiable with just about every American even though our government has done very little about it. Because the number one mandate of the Federal government is our defense, to not secure our borders is either criminal negligence or the most profound incompetence.

The next biggest issue after securing the border is what to do with those who are here illegally. This is not a tolerable situation either—for them and for citizens. This is an especially difficult issue for our Hispanic citizens. The following are some of the main factors why this must be addressed now:

➢ Crime committed by illegal immigrants across the nation is rising, but in border towns and cities, it has become intolerable.

➢ Crime committed against illegal immigrants is rising. They are viewed as easy prey because they are afraid to report crimes to law enforcement.

➢ The social costs of caring for illegal immigrants is a burden most cities and states can no longer bear.

➢ Al Qaeda and Hamas have expanding operations in South and Central America with the intent of training and slipping terrorists into the U.S. among the illegal immigrants, with many likely to have already entered this way.

➢ The failure of the government to secure our borders is eroding American's confidence in their government to fulfill its most basic responsibility to defend us.

➢ Failure to enforce immigration laws is eroding the respect for law and our government.

Why this issue is not being addressed:

➢ Some leaders in large American cities have said that if all of the illegal immigrants were sent home, it would virtually shut down their cities.

➢ Many industries are claiming the same.

➢ Because the birthrate of Americans has dropped below that which can sustain a culture, without high immigration numbers, the domestic economy could be in jeopardy of permanent recession.

➢ This is a political hot potato, and it seems our leaders have not had the courage to deal with an issue in which there is no easy solution, and will likely cost them support regardless of which side they take.

➢ Both major political parties in America have reasons for not wanting to solve this problem, which we will address in more detail below.

With the present job crisis, it is understandable that many Americans think illegal immigrants are taking American jobs. This is likely true in some cases, but it is rare even in the present struggling economy. Illegal immigrants do the work that very few citizens want to do or are willing to do. Once we do what is necessary to get the economy going again, we will have a different kind of job problem—we're not going to have enough people for the jobs we need done. The illegal immigrants are not only willing to do the jobs most citizens do not want to do; they do them much better because they appreciate any job.

Even so, keeping them illegal is not an option. Neither is giving them a cheap path to citizenship. Keeping them illegal weakens our laws, and giving them a cheap, easy path to citizenship devalues American citizenship. There has to be another way, and there is.

Most illegal immigrants just want to provide for their families and tend to be even more law-abiding than citizens because of their fear of exposure for being illegal. One thing we need to do is exchange this fear for a respect for the opportunity they are given to work here. They can be given guest worker status under the condition that this status will be revoked for any serious crime committed, or for failure to pay for their health coverage so that they do not have to overburden our emergency rooms for treatment, and so forth. Serious and enforced penalties for hiring illegal immigrants could greatly discourage, if not virtually eliminate, their hiring after this is implemented.

This problem is not too hard to solve, but the main reason it hasn't been is because of politics. The Democratic Party seems to have secured the allegiance of the majority of Latino citizens at this time simply because they reached out to them and showed sympathy for their causes. However, this is not a natural alliance. A reason why the Democratic Party continues to promise to resolve the illegal-immigration issue but fails to do so could be because their party is the great beneficiary of this controversy as long as they can keep it one. They also know very well that about 90% of the Latino immigrants, both legal and illegal, are pro-life, pro-family, and natural conservatives. Latinos would be much more at home with political conservatives if they were not so threatened by them. If they become citizens and are no longer threatened, many will likely become Republicans.

Victims of Incompetence

In a time when the victim mentality is greatly overplayed, in the case of illegal immigrants it probably is not. Most illegal immigrants would have come in legally if it were possible to get past our broken immigration system. There are qualified applicants who have been in line for ten years or more for a green card. The truth is our country has needed these workers, and they need us, and we need to get this problem corrected.

Hispanic immigrants are not asking for special treatment and are willing to get in the back of the line to become legal if only the line would move! With the automation we have now, there is no reason why any applicant for immigration or guest worker status should have to wait more than ten days for approval. This is just another case of government bureaucratic mismanagement, inefficiency, and incompetence.

A New America

No doubt many undesirables are now getting into the United States through our unsecured borders, but most coming over are not. They are wonderful people who love their families enough to risk all that they do so that they can provide for them. We need immigration reform now that will continue to let us draw from the strengths of those coming, which will also be a filter that keeps out those we don't need.

Immigration to America is not a right but a privilege. This needs to be highlighted by a working immigration system. It is also a privilege for America to receive so many who come with a fresh zeal for freedom and opportunity. This helps keep us constantly renewing. It also challenges the slothful among us, or those who have lost a sense of the blessings we have, and often gets them moving again.

We are enriched by the different cultures, and we should want to assimilate those coming from other countries who want to live in freedom. Even so, anyone wanting American citizenship should also want to be Americans first. To stay moored to the foundations that our country is built on, and that will keep us, there has to be a devotion of those coming to become Americans, honoring what America is, while America also honors their history and culture.

The Chemistry of Renewal

In chemistry, if two substances with opposing characteristics are mixed, there will likely be an explosion, fire, or some form of violence. After this, a new substance emerges with different properties than either of the two original chemicals. Likewise, when races and cultures meet and begin to mix, there will almost always be commotion, and sometimes violence, but what ultimately emerges can be extraordinary, wonderful, and new.

Much of the strength of America has come from this meeting and mixing together of races and cultures to form a nation like no other in many ways. The high degree of innovation, which is such a prevalent gift in America, can be traced to this.

Something new can be born when opposites clash, but to preserve the new thing, we must have a vessel that can contain the violence of the clash. America has proven to be such a strong vessel. This has given birth to many new social elements and makes America one of the most dynamic and interesting places in the world to live, fraught with potential for new ideas, creations, movements, and adventure. This is a major factor behind the prosperity of America.

The immigration problem must be solved, but we must also keep the flow of so much life and vitality coming with this opportunity. We should never take for granted the blessing of having so many wanting to come to America and for what they bring.

CHAPTER TWENTY-ONE
HONORING THE ELDERLY

One of Winston Churchill's best-known quotes is, "If you're not a liberal at twenty, you have no heart; if you're not a conservative at forty, you have no brain." This was true in my life, but things are changing. Studies reveal that even though 85% of college professors are liberals, almost 60% of students are conservatives. The youth are far more educated now and are getting their education from a large number of sources, not just school. They think more for themselves and are questioning the typical inculcation with liberal principles that has been imposed on our students for a couple of generations now. It's almost as if they're rebelling now by being conservative!

When I was young, I was not that smart. I was more than a liberal—I was a radical. I thought liberals were compromisers. I could not comprehend how anyone could be a conservative, and now I am one. Now it is hard for me to comprehend how anyone could be a liberal, much less a progressive (the term today for a more radical liberal). Then I remember how I once was. In my heart, I am still a liberal in many ways, but in my head, I am a conservative. I still share the goals of many liberals, especially making life better for the poor and oppressed, but the evidence is too overwhelming that the government cannot be the means to get that accomplished.

It was also a revelation when the financial statements of our wealthy liberal politicians revealed how consistently little they give to charity compared to their conservative counterparts. Any thinking person has to wonder about that. Is it that the liberals want the government to take care of the issues they do not want to personally get involved with or have to pay for? To expect the government to do everything and fix everyone is now perceived by many more people as the copout that it is. Liberals are now viewed by many as just wanting to tax all of us to do what they themselves do not want to give their own resources to do. I'm not quite that cynical, but I understand why many are.

Personally, I doubt anyone has perfect motives, even for the best things that are done. People can have 90% evil motives for doing something, and 10% good, and think their motives are good because of the 10%. Likewise, some of the most evil people in the world may still have some good motives, but often this only allows them to use the tiny percentage of good in their hearts to justify the evil.

Some basically evil people have done surprisingly good things. Napoleon seemed to think little of the hundreds of thousands who died in battle because of his vanities. However, he cared so much about justice for the common people that he developed a system of justice that the greatest justice systems in the world borrowed from, including America.

For this reason, and because I am not able to know what is in other people's minds or hearts, I assume the best motives in other people, and try to judge the issues on their own merits. If the issue has merit, I then figure out the most efficient, effective way to get there.

Some issues are worthy to take up regardless of the cost. In both the Old and New Testaments, there is only one commandment with a promise—to honor our fathers and mothers. The promise is that if we will do this, then it will "go well with us," and our days will be long in the land the Lord has given to us (see Exodus 20:12). This is the right thing to do. If we are a great society, then we will want the senior years of our elders to be some of their best years, with as much security, peace, and comfort as possible.

Any nation or culture that stops honoring and valuing its elders is in the twilight of its existence. Taking care of our children and our elders is something we must do, and it should be thought of as something very special that we get to do.

Fixing Social Security

Virtually everyone knows that Social Security is heading for a crisis where it will not be able to pay its obligations to citizens. These citizens have paid a large amount of their hard-earned money into it their whole working lives. We do not have to fail them. With some basic good management, Social Security can be saved, and not only pay every obligation it has, but do even much better for the coming generations. However, we can't get to where we want to go if we do not know where we are, so let's take a brief look at where Social Security is.

Social Security is often referred to as an entitlement, but it isn't. It's not an entitlement when people pay their money in and just expect to get their money out when they retire, which is the case with Social Security. It is true that many will get more out of this than they put in, but most will not. This is not an entitlement, but money owed by our government just as much as it owes for any bond. Social Security does need to be fixed, but we need to start with the fact that not paying this to those who have paid it in all of their working lives is simply not an option.

It was reported recently that a popular governor called Social Security a sham, actually saying it was the biggest "Ponzi scheme" in history. He is right on both counts, and it is refreshing to finally hear a politician say this. If you do the simple math, you will see it has been the biggest rip-off in history, and it actually was designed to work just like a Ponzi scheme.

Ponzi was an actual person who was the "Bernie Madoff" of the early 20th century. His scheme paid huge dividends to the early investors but was dependent on an increasing number of new investors whose money was used to pay the earlier ones. When the number of new investors leveled off or started to decrease, the scheme crashed and was revealed for what it was. Ponzi was then arrested because this was obviously criminal. Then our government actually used this principle for our Social Security system. They knew that as long as the population continued to grow fast, there would be enough to pay the early investors in the system.

No one foresaw a day when people would be living so much longer and therefore drawing from the system so much longer, or that the population would level off and there would be fewer people paying into it. Now we're there.

We have to think that if the SEC had been there to examine this system in the beginning, they would have made it clear that they would have thrown anyone into jail who would try to pull off something like this. Many Federal programs should be referred to as schemes and would get anyone in the private sector who did such things a long prison term. Making our government abide by some of these basic rules everyone else has to live by would go a long way into fixing some of the major mismanagement in government. Much of it would be criminal if it were not the government doing it, but it should be.

So the scheme has now been revealed for exactly what it was—a legalized Federal government Ponzi scheme. Now there are fewer people coming into the system. So you either have to take more from each one coming in or give less to those who are now due for their payout. Raising the age of those who can collect corrects it a little bit for a little while, but that too only minimally pushes back the ultimate day of reckoning, which could come in the next Presidential term. Now we're at the time when this has to be fixed. The good news is that it still can be.

Our Social Security system can still be saved without failing to pay all of its obligations and without charging more to those coming into the system. If this is true, why have others not seen it? They have, but they get shouted down for attacking the elderly every time they bring it up. Like most of the answers to almost all of our biggest problems, the solutions are really not that complicated. Like most of the solutions, it has to do with cutting out the waste and bringing in good management. There would have to be adjustments going forward, but the program could be much better, not worse.

Of course, just as Walter Mondale once asked Gary Hart, "Where's the beef?" we could ask, "Where's the math?" This is a legitimate question, and though we can't include all of the math in a short book like this, we will address some of the basic factors.

First, we must establish the principle that for the sake of the most basic honor of the U.S. government, we must pay to everyone everything that our citizens have put into this system. This has to be non-negotiable for the honor of who we are as a nation and because it is the right thing to do. A growing percentage of Americans who now pay into the Social Security system doubt that they will ever see their money again. It should never be that our citizens would lose so much respect and trust in their government. This trust must be restored.

The Greatest Mathematical Equation

Einstein called the principle of compound interest the most important mathematical equation. In just a few more minutes, you will understand why he said this. First, we'll look at a couple of brief, and necessarily dramatized, illustrations.

You have probably been asked a question such as, "What would you take if offered a million dollars or the results of starting with a penny and doubling it every day for a month?" If you took the penny, you chose well because you would have $10,737,418.24 if it's a thirty day month, and $21,474.836.48 if it's a thirty-one day month. That's a demonstration of the power of compounding. It's an exaggerated example, but this dramatizes the power of what we're talking about and what the great financial minds have used for a long time to build great fortunes.

Decades ago, our government did a very righteous thing by allowing an individual to set aside up to $2,000 tax deferred per year into a retirement account. If a couple that marries at age 25 started to fund their Individual Retirement Accounts (IRAs) at that time, putting away $2,000 each per year, at age 65 they will have contributed $160,000 to this account, but will have over **$2,000,000** if they get a 10% annual average return on their investment.

If this couple contributed the same amount to Social Security, they would not even have the buying power of the principle they invested into the system. Social Security accounts are not even paid 1%, and since inflation averages much more than that, in your Social Security account you have been losing some of the principle you invest every year in actual buying power.

Many would wonder where you can receive a 10% return. There are many safe investment vehicles that are popular with those having retirement accounts which have had a higher return than this. Some have done much better than this even through the recent turbulence in the markets. There are fund managers who know how to make money in up, down, or sideways markets. You can benefit from their expertise through mutual funds and other investment vehicles. You might think they are too risky because they are not the government, or backed by the FDIC, but there may not be a more riskier investment that you could make right now than to pay into Social Security and let your government manage it.

Now let's go back to the couple who married and started contributing to their IRAs at age 25. If this couple is a little more aggressive with their investments and receives an average of 14% return, they will have almost **$9,000,000** when they reach age 65. If they receive a 16% average return, they will have over **$17,000,000.** This is *$15,000,000* more or over 8 times as much as they would have if they received a 10% average return. This is the power of compound interest over time. Again, the returns:

- 10% = $ 2,000,000
- 14% = $ 9,000.000
- 16% = $17,000,000

How much would you have in your retirement account if you had been able to invest it in a mutual fund instead of Social Security? Almost certainly millions. It is time to demand the kind of change that will make this a true benefit and to recognize the robbery of the American people who have been misled into thinking it has been a benefit. Remember, this is not the government's money, and it is not an entitlement—it is your money! It came out of your pocket and was deducted from your paycheck.

If what has been done to the American people could be any worse, it does get worse. Not only have they so poorly managed your retirement account that you have received less than 1% interest on your money, but they have also taken all of the money out of your account! There is nothing in the "lockbox" of Social Security but government IOU's. Certainly our government will be able to pay these we may think, but no one in government right now has been able to figure out how.

With government deficits now running in the trillions of dollars a year, it is understandable that fewer people ever expect to get any of the money they put into Social Security. Far too many are counting on this for their retirement and will have little or no other sources of income in their senior years. Just a few years ago it was projected that this crisis would hit around 2050 with the government not being able to pay Social Security benefits. With the mushrooming Federal deficits, it is now projected to hit as early as 2016.

Of course, many are saying this is the reason why the present Administration keeps trying to slip the end-of-life counseling provision into the healthcare reform legislation. We must resolve that we will honor our fathers and mothers, and whatever it takes we will never abandon the great generation who worked and fought so hard to deliver to us such a great country.

A Solution

The looming Social Security crisis will be the biggest social crisis in our history if not addressed soon. President George W. Bush tried to deal with this and the screams from those feigning to be protecting the rights of the elderly got so shrill he was forced to back off. Bush's plan for saving Social Security may not have been perfect, but his proposals would already have it in much better shape than it is now.

Again, our integrity demands that our citizens get what they have been promised. This can only be accomplished by doing what was proposed at the beginning of this book—cut the size and cost of the Federal government down to what it should be. This would free up trillions of dollars over the next few years, some of which should go to paying back Social Security for what has been borrowed from it. If the government wants to borrow from Social Security again, it should issue bonds to it at the going interest rate with a guaranteed floor that at least covers inflation.

If this rule had been applied at the beginning of the government's pillaging of the Social Security funds, it is likely that every recipient today would be getting at least twice as much in their Social Security checks as they are now.

We have to do the right thing, and the citizens who have contributed to Social Security must be given what they have been promised. Our Founding Fathers risked their lives, their fortunes, and their sacred honor to lay the foundation for this great country, and the sacred honor of this nation has to mean that it will make good on its promises.

Social Security should be managed by the highest standards of excellence, efficiency, and accountability for the sake of those who trust so much of their resources and futures to the government. There should also be an option for those who would like to invest at least a portion of their money in this account in vehicles that can bring higher rates of return. The options allowed could be those that are rated for safety and performance.

Medicare can be fixed by many of the same issues previously discussed that solve the problems with healthcare. The intent of these programs is not wrong as much as their design and management have been so poor. A good argument can be made that the government should not be in these types of programs anyway, but that we should just have a closely regulated private industry doing this. Perhaps.

"Thank You Uncle Sam"

As complex and outrageous as some of our tax policies can be, in some ways it does reward biblical righteousness. In His "Parable of the Talents" the Lord taught that the "good and faithful servant" was the one who managed well the resources entrusted to him. Likewise the "wicked evil slave" was the one do did not manage well what was entrusted to (see Matthew 25:21-26). Our tax polices reward those willing take a little time and make a little effort to learn to manage their resources, taking advantage of things like IRAs and other retirement accounts.

We discussed how much difference just a few percentage points can make over time because of compound interest. Now consider this: Just by allowing you to defer taxes on what you deposit into these accounts, the government is giving you a basic 15% return on this money if you are in the 15% tax bracket. If you are in the 35% bracket, the government is giving you a 35% return up front just by not making you pay taxes on it until you start drawing it out. For this reason, having and using a retirement account is basic to good personal management of our resources, and we can thank the government for programs like this that encourage us to save on our own, and pay us very well to do it!

CHAPTER TWENTY-TWO

THE GREAT AMERICAN RENEWAL

The more insecure someone is about their authority, the more rigid, domineering, and controlling they will tend to be to compensate for their insecurity. This is likewise true of governments—the truly great, and truly strong, will not be overly rigid or overly controlling.

America has had many highs and lows in her history. What is it about America that enables her to stay so flexible and to keep renewing herself as she does? To a large degree, this is the result of the principles America was founded on. These principles have enabled such a large and powerful nation to be strong while also remarkably nimble.

The most basic of these principles that are the core values of America is freedom. Even though our founding principles promote such individualism and liberty, they also promote the individual responsibility to compel us to bond together in crises, or respond to other nations who need us. They have also been an effective compass for navigating through the difficulties we've encountered, and to date, they have never failed to get us to a safe harbor in the storm.

Summary

Most of what I have shared has necessarily been generalizations. I have not used footnotes and references to some of the studies in the book for two reasons. First, I want what is proposed to stand on its own merit. Second, I didn't have time to do this.

Talking theory like this is far easier than actually taking on the job of bringing such proposed radical changes. However, we are at the place where we can no longer delay. This must be done or we will soon lose our economy, our political system, and our way of life. You know this is true. It will take the same kind of courage, boldness, and willingness to sacrifice to save our country as it did to found it.

I run an organization now that has employed up to two hundred people directly and many more indirectly. It's a ministry, and over the last few years we've seen contributions dip as could be expected in such difficult times. Like most, we've had to make deep cutbacks and still have needed miracles to make our payrolls. Hardly a day goes by when I don't think of all the families depending on us. I've watched our people, who are missionaries, and many are only making a fraction of what they could probably make in business, and yet I would have to implement pay cuts. Almost all took it so cheerfully that I have hardly ever heard of a complaint. There is no way for me to communicate how much I appreciate these people, and this only made me care even more to do the best job for them that I can. I can honestly say there are times when I think I would have rather amputated an arm than lay them off or cut their pay. Most employers I know feel this way about their people.

Now think about George Washington and his army. They went for three years with no pay. Often they had no food. They marched through the snow with burlap bags wrapped around their feet because they did not even have shoes. They suffered like this for us, and the only reward many of them ever received was to go toe-to-toe with the most powerful army in the world at the time and probably die. It took that kind of willing sacrifice to give birth to this country, and many more have made a similar sacrifice to preserve it. Now it is our time. We cannot let the country that so many great souls paid such a high price for be lost on our watch. That is not an option.

The solutions to many of our ultimate problems are simple and easy to understand, but that does not mean they are going to be easy to implement. It is once again going to take an extraordinary leadership with uncommon vision, courage, and resolve. Can we count you in?

ADDENDUM
SOLZHENITSYN'S HARVARD SPEECH

Text of Address by

**Alexander Solzhenitsyn
at Harvard Class Day Afternoon Exercises,
Thursday, June 8, 1978**

I am sincerely happy to be here with you on this occasion and to become personally acquainted with this old and most prestigious University. My congratulations and very best wishes to all of today's graduates.

Harvard's motto is "Veritas." Many of you have already found out and others will find out in the course of their lives that truth eludes us if we do not concentrate with total attention on its pursuit. And even while it eludes us, the illusion still lingers of knowing it and leads to many misunderstandings. Also, truth is seldom pleasant; it is almost invariably bitter. There is some bitterness in my speech today, too. But I want to stress that it comes not from an adversary but from a friend.

Three years ago in the United States I said certain things which at that time appeared unacceptable. Today, however, many people agree with what I then said....

A World Split Apart
by Alexander Solzhenitsyn

The split in today's world is perceptible even to a hasty glance. Any of our contemporaries readily identifies two world powers, each

185

of them already capable of entirely destroying the other. However, understanding of the split often is limited to this political conception, to the illusion that danger may be abolished through successful diplomatic negotiations or by achieving a balance of armed forces. The truth is that the split is a much profounder and a more alienating one, that the rifts are more than one can see at first glance. This deep manifold split bears the danger of manifold disaster for all of us, in accordance with the ancient truth that a Kingdom— in this case, our Earth—divided against itself cannot stand.

Contemporary Worlds

There is the concept of the Third World: thus, we already have three worlds. Undoubtedly, however, the number is even greater; we are just too far away to see. Any ancient deeply rooted autonomous culture, especially if it is spread on a wide part of the earth's surface, constitutes an autonomous world, full of riddles and surprises to Western thinking. As a minimum, we must include in this category China, India, the Muslim world and Africa, if indeed we accept the approximation of viewing the latter two as compact units. For one thousand years Russia has belonged to such a category, although Western thinking systematically committed the mistake of denying its autonomous character and therefore never understood it, just as today the West does not understand Russia in communist captivity. It may be that in the past years Japan has increasingly become a distant part of the West, I am no judge here; but as to Israel, for instance, it seems to me that it stands apart from the Western world in that its state system is fundamentally linked to religion.

How short a time ago, relatively, the small new European world was easily seizing colonies everywhere, not only without anticipating any real resistance, but also usually despising any possible values in the conquered peoples' approach to life. On the face of it, it was an overwhelming success; there were no geographic frontiers to it. Western society expanded in a triumph of human independence and power. And all of a sudden in the 20th century came the discovery of its fragility and friability. We now see that the conquests proved to be short lived and precarious, and this in turn points to defects in the Western view of the world which led to these conquests. Relations with the former colonial world now have turned into their opposite and the Western world often goes to extremes of obsequiousness, but it is difficult yet to estimate the total size of the bill which former colonial countries will present to the West, and it is difficult to predict whether the surrender not only of its last colonies, but of everything it owns will be sufficient for the West to foot the bill.

Convergence

But the blindness of superiority continues in spite of all and upholds the belief that vast regions everywhere on our planet should develop and mature to the level of present day Western systems which in theory are the best and in practice the most attractive. There is this belief that all those other worlds are only being temporarily prevented by wicked governments or by heavy crises or by their own barbarity or incomprehension from taking the way of Western pluralistic democracy and from adopting the Western way of life. Countries are judged on the merit of their progress in this direction. However, it is a conception which developed out of Western incomprehension of the essence of other worlds, out of the mistake of measuring them all with a Western yardstick. The real picture of our planet's development is quite different.

Anguish about our divided world gave birth to the theory of convergence between leading Western countries and the Soviet Union. It is a soothing theory which overlooks the fact that these worlds are not at all developing into similarity; neither one can be transformed into the other without the use of violence. Besides, convergence inevitably means acceptance of the other side's defects, too, and this is hardly desirable.

If I were today addressing an audience in my country, examining the overall pattern of the world's rifts I would have concentrated on the East's calamities. But since my forced exile in the West has now lasted four years and since my audience is a Western one, I think it may be of greater interest to concentrate on certain aspects of the West in our days, such as I see them.

A Decline in Courage [. . .]

may be the most striking feature which an outside observer notices in the West in our days. The Western world has lost its civil courage, both as a whole and separately, in each country, each government, each political party and of course in the United Nations. Such a decline in courage is particularly noticeable among the ruling groups and the intellectual elite, causing an impression of loss of courage by the entire society. Of course, there are many courageous individuals but they have no determining influence on public life. Political and intellectual bureaucrats show depression, passivity and perplexity in their actions and in their statements and even more so in theoretical reflections to explain how realistic, reasonable as well as intellectually and even morally warranted it is to base state policies on weakness and cowardice. And decline in courage is ironically emphasized by occasional explosions of anger and inflexibility on the part of the same bureaucrats when dealing with weak governments and weak countries, not supported by anyone, or with currents which cannot offer any resistance. But they get tongue-tied and paralyzed when they deal with powerful governments and threatening forces, with aggressors and international terrorists.

Should one point out that from ancient times decline in courage has been considered the beginning of the end?

Well-Being

When the modern Western States were created, the following principle was proclaimed: governments are meant to serve man, and man lives to be free to pursue happiness. (See, for example, the American Declaration.) Now at last during past decades technical and social progress has permitted the realization of such aspirations: the welfare state. Every citizen has been granted the desired freedom and material goods in such quantity and of such quality as to guarantee in theory the achievement of happiness, in the morally inferior sense which has come into being during those same decades. In the process, however, one psychological detail has been overlooked: the constant desire to have still more things and a still better life and the struggle to obtain them imprints many Western faces with worry and even depression, though it is customary to conceal such feelings. Active and tense competition permeates all human thoughts without opening a way to free spiritual development. The individual's independence from many types of state pressure has been guaranteed; the majority of people have been granted well-being to an extent their fathers and grandfathers could not even dream about; it has become possible to raise young people according to these ideals, leading them to physical splendor, happiness, possession of material goods, money and leisure, to an almost unlimited freedom of enjoyment. So who should now renounce all this, why and for what should one risk one's precious life in defense of common values, and particularly in such nebulous cases when the security of one's nation must be defended in a distant country?

Even biology knows that habitual extreme safety and well-being are not advantageous for a living organism. Today, well-being in the life of Western society has begun to reveal its pernicious mask.

Legalistic Life

Western society has given itself the organization best suited to its purposes, based, I would say, on the letter of the law. The limits of human rights and righteousness are determined by a system of laws; such limits are very broad. People in the West have acquired considerable skill in using, interpreting and manipulating law, even though laws tend to be too complicated for an average person to understand without the help of an expert. Any conflict is solved according to the letter of the law and this is considered to be the supreme solution. If one is right from a legal point of view, nothing more is required, nobody may mention that one could still not be entirely right, and urge self-restraint, a willingness to renounce such legal rights, sacrifice and selfless risk: it would sound simply absurd.

189

One almost never sees voluntary self-restraint. Everybody operates at the extreme limit of those legal frames. An oil company is legally blameless when it purchases an invention of a new type of energy in order to prevent its use. A food product manufacturer is legally blameless when he poisons his produce to make it last longer: after all, people are free not to buy it.

I have spent all my life under a communist regime and I will tell you that a society without any objective legal scale is a terrible one indeed. But a society with no other scale but the legal one is not quite worthy of man either. A society which is based on the letter of the law and never reaches any higher is taking very scarce advantage of the high level of human possibilities. The letter of the law is too cold and formal to have a beneficial influence on society. Whenever the tissue of life is woven of legalistic relations, there is an atmosphere of moral mediocrity, paralyzing man's noblest impulses.

And it will be simply impossible to stand through the trials of this threatening century with only the support of a legalistic structure.

The Direction of Freedom

In today's Western society, the inequality has been revealed of freedom for good deeds and freedom for evil deeds. A statesman who wants to achieve something important and highly constructive for his country has to move cautiously and even timidly; there are thousands of hasty and irresponsible critics around him, parliament and the press keep rebuffing him. As he moves ahead, he has to prove that every single step of his is well-founded and absolutely flawless. Actually an outstanding and particularly gifted person who has unusual and unexpected initiatives in mind hardly gets a chance to assert himself; from the very beginning, dozens of traps will be set out for him. Thus mediocrity triumphs with the excuse of restrictions imposed by democracy.

It is feasible and easy everywhere to undermine administrative power and, in fact, it has been drastically weakened in all Western countries. The defense of individual rights has reached such extremes as to make society as a whole defenseless against certain individuals. It is time, in the West, to defend not so much human rights as human obligations.

Destructive and irresponsible freedom has been granted boundless space. Society appears to have little defense against the abyss of human decadence, such as, for example, misuse of liberty for moral violence against young people, motion pictures full of pornography, crime and horror. It is considered to be part of freedom and theoretically counter-balanced by the young people's right not to look or not to accept. Life organized legalistically has thus shown its inability to defend itself against the corrosion of evil.

And what shall we say about the dark realm of criminality as such? Legal frames (especially in the United States) are broad enough to encourage not only individual freedom but also certain individual crimes. The culprit can go unpunished or obtain undeserved leniency with the support of thousands of public defenders. When a government starts an earnest fight against terrorism, public opinion immediately accuses it of violating the terrorists' civil rights. There are many such cases.

Such a tilt of freedom in the direction of evil has come about gradually but it was evidently born primarily out of a humanistic and benevolent concept according to which there is no evil inherent to human nature; the world belongs to mankind and all the defects of life are caused by wrong social systems which must be corrected. Strangely enough, though the best social conditions have been achieved in the West, there still is criminality and there even is considerably more of it than in the pauper and lawless Soviet society. (There is a huge number of prisoners in our camps which are termed criminals, but most of them never committed any crime; they merely tried to defend themselves against a lawless state resorting to means outside of a legal framework.)

The Direction of the Press

The press too, of course, enjoys the widest freedom. (I shall be using the word press to include all media.) But what sort of use does it make of this freedom?

Here again, the main concern is not to infringe the letter of the law. There is no moral responsibility for deformation or disproportion. What sort of responsibility does a journalist have to his readers, or to history? If they have misled public opinion or the government by inaccurate information or wrong conclusions, do we know of any cases of public recognition and rectification of such mistakes by the same journalist or the same newspaper? No, it does not happen, because it would damage sales. A nation may be the victim of such a mistake, but the journalist always gets away with it. One may safely assume that he will start writing the opposite with renewed self-assurance.

Because instant and credible information has to be given, it becomes necessary to resort to guesswork, rumors and suppositions to fill in the voids, and none of them will ever be rectified, they will stay on in the readers' memory. How many hasty, immature, superficial and misleading judgments are expressed every day, confusing readers, without any verification. The press can both simulate public opinion and miseducate it. Thus we may see terrorists heroized, or secret matters, pertaining to one's nation's defense, publicly revealed, or we may witness shameless intrusion on the privacy of well-known people under the slogan: "Everyone is entitled to know everything." But this is a false slogan, characteristic of a false era: people also have the right not to know, and it is a much more valuable one. The right not to have their divine souls stuffed with gossip, nonsense, vain talk. A person who works and leads a meaningful life does not need this excessive burdening flow of information.

Hastiness and superficiality are the psychic disease of the 20th century and more than anywhere else this disease is reflected in the press. In-depth analysis of a problem is anathema to the press. It stops at sensational formulas.

Such as it is, however, the press has become the greatest power within the Western countries, more powerful than the legislature, the executive and the judiciary. One would then like to ask: by what law has it been elected and to whom is it responsible? In the communist East a journalist is frankly appointed as a state official. But who has granted Western journalists their power, for how long a time and with what prerogatives?

There is yet another surprise for someone coming from the East where the press is rigorously unified: One gradually discovers a common trend of preferences within the Western press as a whole. It is a fashion; there are generally accepted patterns of judgment and there may be common corporate interests, the sum effect being not competition but unification. Enormous freedom exists for the press, but not for the readership because newspapers mostly give enough stress and emphasis to those opinions which do not too openly contradict their own and the general trend.

A Fashion in Thinking

Without any censorship, in the West fashionable trends of thought and ideas are carefully separated from those which are not fashionable; nothing is forbidden, but what is not fashionable will hardly ever find its way into periodicals or books or be heard in colleges. Legally your researchers are free, but they are conditioned by the fashion of the day. There is no open violence such as in the East; however, a selection dictated by fashion and the need to match mass standards frequently prevent independent-minded people from giving their contribution to public life. There is a dangerous tendency to form a herd, shutting off successful development. I have received letters in America from highly intelligent persons, maybe a teacher in a faraway small college who could do much for the renewal and salvation of his country, but his country cannot hear him because the media are not interested in him. This gives birth to strong mass prejudices, blindness, which is most dangerous in our dynamic era. There is, for instance, a self-deluding interpretation of the contemporary world situation. It works as a sort of petrified armor around people's minds. Human voices from 17 countries of Eastern Europe and Eastern Asia cannot pierce it. It will only be broken by the pitiless crowbar of events.

I have mentioned a few trends of Western life which surprise and shock a new arrival to this world. The purpose and scope of this speech will not allow me to continue such a review, to look into the influence of these Western characteristics on important aspects on [the] nation's life, such as elementary education, advanced education in....

Socialism

It is almost universally recognized that the West shows all the world a way to successful economic development, even though in the past years it has been strongly disturbed by chaotic inflation. However, many people living in the West are dissatisfied with their own society. They despise it or accuse it of not being up to the level of maturity attained by mankind. A number of such critics turn to socialism, which is a false and dangerous current.

I hope that no one present will suspect me of offering my personal criticism of the Western system to present socialism as an alternative. Having experienced applied socialism in a country where the alternative has been realized, I certainly will not speak for it. The well-known Soviet mathematician Shafarevich, a member of the Soviet Academy of Science, has written a brilliant book under the title *Socialism*; it is a profound analysis showing that socialism of any type and shade leads to a total destruction of the human spirit and to a leveling of mankind into death. Shafarevich's book was published in France almost two years ago and so far no one has been found to refute it. It will shortly be published in English in the United States.

Not a Model

But should someone ask me whether I would indicate the West such as it is today as a model to my country, frankly I would have to answer negatively. No, I could not recommend your society in its present state as an ideal for the transformation of ours. Through intense suffering our country has now achieved a spiritual development of such intensity that the Western system in its present state of spiritual exhaustion does not look attractive. Even those characteristics of your life which I have just mentioned are extremely saddening.

A fact which cannot be disputed is the weakening of human beings in the West while in the East they are becoming firmer and stronger. Six decades for our people and three decades for the people of Eastern Europe; during that time we have been through a spiritual training far in advance of Western experience. Life's complexity and mortal weight have produced stronger, deeper and more interesting characters than those produced by standardized Western well-being. Therefore if our society were to be transformed into yours, it would mean an improvement in certain aspects, but also a change for the worse on some particularly significant scores. It is true, no doubt, that a society cannot remain in an abyss of lawlessness, as is the case in our country. But it is also demeaning for it to elect such mechanical legalistic smoothness as you have. After the suffering of decades of violence and oppression, the human soul longs for things higher, warmer and purer than those offered by today's mass living habits, introduced by the revolting invasion of publicity, by TV stupor and by intolerable music.

All this is visible to observers from all the worlds of our planet. The Western way of life is less and less likely to become the leading model.

There are meaningful warnings that history gives a threatened or perishing society. Such are, for instance, the decadence of art, or a lack of great statesmen. There are open and evident warnings, too. The center of your democracy and of your culture is left without electric power for a few hours only, and all of a sudden crowds of American citizens start looting and creating havoc. The smooth surface film must be very thin, then, the social system quite unstable and unhealthy.

But the fight for our planet, physical and spiritual, a fight of cosmic proportions, is not a vague matter of the future; it has already started. The forces of Evil have begun their decisive offensive, you can feel their pressure, and yet your screens and publications are full of prescribed smiles and raised glasses. What is the joy about?

Shortsightedness

Very well known representatives of your society, such as George Kennan, say: we cannot apply moral criteria to politics. Thus we mix good and evil, right and wrong and make space for the absolute triumph of absolute Evil in the world. On the contrary, only moral criteria can help the West against communism's well planned world strategy. There are no other criteria. Practical or occasional considerations of any kind will inevitably be swept away by strategy. After a certain level of the problem has been reached, legalistic thinking induces paralysis; it prevents one from seeing the size and meaning of events.

In spite of the abundance of information, or maybe because of it, the West has difficulties in understanding reality such as it is. There have been naive predictions by some American experts who believed that Angola would become the Soviet Union's Vietnam or that Cuban expeditions in Africa would best be stopped by special U.S. courtesy to Cuba. Kennan's advice to his own country—to begin unilateral disarmament—belongs to the same category. If you only knew how the youngest of the Moscow Old Square [1] officials laugh at your political wizards! As to Fidel Castro, he frankly scorns the United States, sending his troops to distant adventures from his country right next to yours.

However, the most cruel mistake occurred with the failure to understand the Vietnam war. Some people sincerely wanted all wars to stop just as soon as possible; others believed that there should be room for national, or communist, self-determination in Vietnam, or in Cambodia, as we see today with particular clarity. But members of the U.S. anti-war movement wound up being involved in the betrayal of Far Eastern nations, in a genocide and in the suffering today imposed on 30 million people there. Do those convinced pacifists hear the moans coming from there? Do they understand their responsibility today? Or do they prefer not to hear? The American Intelligentsia lost its [nerve] and as a consequence thereof danger has come much closer to the United States. But there is no awareness of this. Your shortsighted politicians who signed the hasty Vietnam capitulation seemingly gave America a carefree breathing pause; however, a hundredfold Vietnam now looms over you. That small Vietnam had been a warning and an occasion to mobilize the nation's courage. But if a full-fledged America suffered a real defeat from a small communist half-country, how can the West hope to stand firm in the future?

I have had occasion already to say that in the 20th century democracy has not won any major war without help and protection from a powerful continental ally whose philosophy and ideology it did not question. In World War II against Hitler, instead of winning that war with its own forces, which would certainly have been sufficient, Western democracy grew and cultivated another enemy who would prove worse and more powerful yet, as Hitler never had so many resources and so many people, nor did he offer any attractive ideas, or have such a large number of supporters in the West—a potential fifth column—as the Soviet Union. At present, some Western voices already have spoken of obtaining protection from a third power against aggression in the next world conflict, if there is one; in this case the shield would be China. But I would not wish such an outcome to any country in the world. First of all, it is again a doomed alliance with Evil; also, it would grant the United States a respite, but when at a later date China with its billion people would turn around armed with American weapons, America itself would fall prey to a genocide similar to the one perpetrated in Cambodia in our days.

Loss of Willpower

And yet—no weapons, no matter how powerful, can help the West until it overcomes its loss of willpower. In a state of psychological weakness, weapons become a burden for the capitulating side. To defend oneself, one must also be ready to die; there is little such readiness in a society raised in the cult of material well-being. Nothing is left, then, but concessions, attempts to gain time and betrayal. Thus at the shameful Belgrade conference free Western diplomats in their weakness surrendered the line where enslaved members of Helsinki watch groups are sacrificing their lives.

Western thinking has become conservative: the world situation should stay as it is at any cost, there should be no changes. This debilitating dream of a status quo is the symptom of a society which has come to the end of its development. But one must be blind in order not to see that oceans no longer belong to the West, while land under its domination keeps shrinking. The two so-called world wars (they were by far not on a world scale, not yet) have meant internal self-destruction of the small, progressive West which has thus prepared its own end. The next war (which does not have to be an atomic one and I do not believe it will) may well bury Western civilization forever.

Facing such a danger, with such historical values in your past, at such a high level of realization of freedom and apparently of devotion to freedom, how is it possible to lose to such an extent the will to defend oneself?

Humanism and Its Consequences

How has this unfavorable relation of forces come about? How did the West decline from its triumphal march to its present sickness? Have there been fatal turns and losses of direction in its development? It does not seem so. The West kept advancing socially in accordance with its proclaimed intentions, with the help of brilliant technological progress. And all of a sudden it found itself in its present state of weakness.

This means that the mistake must be at the root, at the very basis of human thinking in the past centuries. I refer to the prevailing Western view of the world which was first born during the Renaissance and found its political expression from the period of the Enlightenment. It became the basis for government and social science and could be defined as rationalistic humanism or humanistic autonomy: the proclaimed and enforced autonomy of man from any higher force above him. It could also be called anthropocentricity, with man seen as the center of everything that exists.

The turn introduced by the Renaissance evidently was inevitable historically. The Middle Ages had come to a natural end by exhaustion, becoming an intolerable despotic repression of man's physical nature in favor of the spiritual one. Then, however, we turned our backs upon the Spirit and embraced all that is material with excessive and unwarranted zeal. This new way of thinking, which had imposed on us its guidance, did not admit the existence of intrinsic evil in man nor did it see any higher task than the attainment of happiness on earth. It based modern Western civilization on the dangerous trend to worship man and his material needs. Everything beyond physical well-being and accumulation of material goods, all other human requirements and characteristics of a subtler and higher nature, were left outside the area of attention of state and social systems, as if human life did not have any superior sense. That provided access for evil, of which in our days there is a free and constant flow. Merely freedom does not in the least solve all the problems of human life and it even adds a number of new ones.

However, in early democracies, as in American democracy at the time of its birth, all individual human rights were granted because man is God's creature. That is, freedom was given to the individual conditionally, in the assumption of his constant religious responsibility. Such was the heritage of the preceding thousand years. Two hundred or even fifty years ago, it would have seemed quite impossible, in America, that an individual could be granted boundless freedom simply for the satisfaction of his instincts or whims. Subsequently, however, all such limitations were discarded everywhere in the West; a total liberation occurred from the moral heritage of Christian centuries with their great reserves of mercy and sacrifice. State systems were becoming increasingly and totally materialistic. The West ended up by truly enforcing human rights, sometimes even excessively, but man's sense of responsibility to God and society grew dimmer and dimmer. In the past decades, the legalistically selfish aspect of Western approach and thinking has reached its final dimension and the world wound up in a harsh spiritual crisis and a political impasse. All the glorified technological achievements of Progress, including the conquest of outer space, do not redeem the Twentieth Century's moral poverty which no one could imagine even as late as in the Nineteenth Century.

An Unexpected Kinship

As humanism in its development became more and more materialistic, it made itself increasingly accessible to speculation and manipulation at first by socialism and then by communism. So that Karl Marx was able to say in 1844 that "communism is naturalized humanism."

This statement turned out not to be entirely senseless. One does see the same stones in the foundations of a de-spiritualized humanism and of any type of socialism: endless materialism; freedom from religion and religious responsibility, which under communist regimes reach the stage of anti-religious dictatorship; concentration on social structures with a seemingly scientific approach. (This is typical of the Enlightenment in the Eighteenth Century and of Marxism.) Not by coincidence all of communism's meaningless pledges and oaths are about Man, with a capital M, and his earthly happiness. At first glance it seems an ugly parallel: common traits in the thinking and way of life of today's West and today's East? But such is the logic of materialistic development.

The interrelationship is such, too, that the current of materialism which is most to the left always ends up by being stronger, more attractive and victorious, because it is more consistent. Humanism without its Christian heritage cannot resist such competition. We watch this process in the past centuries and especially in the past decades, on a world scale as the situation becomes increasingly dramatic. Liberalism was inevitably displaced by radicalism, radicalism had to surrender to socialism and socialism could never resist communism. The communist regime in the East could stand and grow due to the enthusiastic support from an enormous number of Western intellectuals who felt a kinship and refused to see communism's crimes. When they no longer could do so, they tried to justify them. In our Eastern countries, communism has suffered a complete ideological defeat; it is zero and less than zero. But Western intellectuals still look at it with interest and with empathy, and this is precisely what makes it so immensely difficult for the West to withstand the East.

Before the Turn

I am not examining here the case of a world war disaster and the changes which it would produce in society. As long as we wake up every morning under a peaceful sun, we have to lead an everyday life. There is a disaster, however, which has already been under way for quite some time. I am referring to the calamity of a de-spiritualized and irreligious humanistic consciousness.

To such consciousness, man is the touchstone in judging and evaluating everything on earth. Imperfect man, who is never free of pride, self-interest, envy, vanity, and dozens of other defects. We are now experiencing the consequences of mistakes which had not been noticed at the beginning of the journey. On the way from the Renaissance to our days we have enriched our experience, but we have lost the concept of a Supreme Complete Entity which used to restrain our passions and our irresponsibility. We have placed too much hope in political and social reforms, only to find out that we were being deprived of our most precious possession: our spiritual life. In the East, it is destroyed by the dealings and machinations of the ruling party. In the West, commercial interests tend to suffocate it. This is the real crisis. The split in the world is less terrible than the similarity of the disease plaguing its main sections.

If humanism were right in declaring that man is born to be happy, he would not be born to die. Since his body is doomed to die, his task on earth evidently must be of a more spiritual nature. It cannot unrestrained enjoyment of everyday life. It cannot be the search for the best ways to obtain material goods and then cheerfully get the most out of them. It has to be the fulfillment of a permanent, earnest duty so that one's life journey may become an experience of moral growth, so that one may leave life a better human being than one started it. It is imperative to review the table of widespread human values. Its present incorrectness is astounding. It is not possible that assessment of the President's performance be reduced to the question of how much money one makes or of unlimited availability of gasoline. Only voluntary, inspired self-restraint can raise man above the world stream of materialism.

It would be retrogression to attach oneself today to the ossified formulas of the Enlightenment. Social dogmatism leaves us completely helpless in front of the trials of our times.

Even if we are spared destruction by war, our lives will have to change if we want to save life from self-destruction. We cannot avoid revising the fundamental definitions of human life and human society. Is it true that man is above everything? Is there no Superior Spirit above him? Is it right that man's life and society's activities have to be determined by material expansion in the first place? Is it permissible to promote such expansion to the detriment of our spiritual integrity?

If the world has not come to its end, it has approached a major turn in history, equal in importance to the turn from the Middle Ages to the Renaissance. It will exact from us a spiritual upsurge, we shall have to rise to a new height of vision, to a new level of life where our physical nature will not be cursed as in the Middle Ages, but, even more importantly, our spiritual being will not be trampled upon as in the Modern era.

This ascension will be similar to climbing onto the next anthropologic stage. No one on earth has any other way left but—upward.

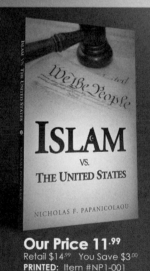

THE OAK INITIATIVE®

Unite. Mobilize. Equip. Activate.

We the People

The Oak Initiative is a grassroots movement to **unite, mobilize, equip,** and **activate** Christians to be the salt and light they are called to become by engaging in the great issues of our time from a sound biblical worldview.

Started by more than 300 Christian leaders from across the spectrum of the body of Christ, within months of its founding, The Oak Initiative had a presence in all 50 states and more than 50 nations, with Oak Gatherings and Oak Chapters springing up rapidly.

FOR MORE INFORMATION, CALL (803)-547-8217

E-mail office@theoakinitiative.org
or
visit us at www.theoakinitiative.org